ETERNAL LOVE

ETERNAL LOVE

Conversations with the LORD in the Heart

His Divine Grace
KĪRTANĀNANDA SWAMI BHAKTIPĀDA

BHAKTIPADA BOOKS

Readers interested in the subject matter of this book are invited to visit the New Vrindaban Community, Home of Prabhupada's Palace of Gold, Hare Krishna Ridge, Moundsville, W.Va., or to correspond with the Secretary.

c/o New Vrindaban
R.D.1, Box 319
Moundsville, W.Va. 26041

2/96

First Printing 25,000 copies

Printed in Singapore

Library of Congress Catalog Card No. 85-073833
ISBN: 0-932215-04-1 Soft cover
     0-932215-06-8 Hard cover

gift

His Divine Grace Kirtanananda Swami Bhaktipada and His Beloved
Spiritual Master, His Divine Grace A.C. Bhaktivedanta Swami
Prabhupada. The loving relationship between the spiritual master
and his disciple is the essence of eternal love.

BOOKS by
His Divine Grace
Kirtanananda Swami Bhaktipada

Song of God — A Summary Study of Bhagavad-gita As It Is

Christ and Krishna — The Path of Pure Devotion

Eternal Love — Conversations with the Lord in the Heart

Rama, The Supreme Personality of Godhead

A complete catalog is available upon request.

Palace Publishing
New Vrindaban Community
RD 1, Box 320
Moundsville, WV 26041

CONTENTS

PART TWO
Conversations With The Lord In The Heart

PART THREE
Chant And Be Happy

PART ONE

Reflections For The
Purification Of The Soul

Meditation 1

Regular Hearing And Service Bring
Detachment From The Material World

"BY REGULARLY HEARING the Word of God and rendering service unto the pure devotee, all that is troublesome to the heart is practically destroyed, and loving service unto the glorious Lord, who is praised with transcendental songs, is established as an irrevocable fact."
(*Srimad-Bhagavatam* 1:2:18)

Here is the remedy for all problems: cleansing the heart of all material contamination by the association of God. Although thought by many to be unattainable, the Lord's association is experienced through two transcendental mediums: His book and His devotee. Both are equally competent to help us. The books of God are full of informative stories and descriptions about the Lord; and the devotee, because he lives a life of perfect harmony with those books, is himself a walking scripture. Since both are the direct, empowered representatives of God, they are equally effective, and we are herein admonished to hear and serve them.

The call to pure devotional service is greater than any other—be it material, philosophical, or metaphysical—for such service immediately opens the heart to the storehouse of Truth. There are, of course, many who do not find the Truth because they are not pure in heart and have not adopted the spirit of submissive inquiry and service necessary to make their search successful.

After all, what good is our show of surrender to the will of God if we lack the sincerity and humility to follow the instructions of His representatives? Indeed, it is not research and erudition that make for holiness but a life of submission to the will of God. In *Bhagavad-gita*, Lord Krishna says that if a sincere soul offers Him even the most insignificant thing—a leaf, a flower, fruit or water—He is satisfied by that offering of love.

What is the profit of knowing all the scriptures by heart if we still do not attain unalloyed love for God? By such love, we can find His grace and mercy perfectly manifest in boundless joy and limitless transcendental knowledge; without this perfect love, however, everything—even penances, austerities, and study of the scriptures—is useless and vain.

Love of God is the first commandment and the greatest wisdom. In practice, love of God means disdain for the things of this present world. Our hearts are now troubled by so many material dreams and desires, which always make us anxious, but we are promised herein that the transcendental medium of submissive hearing will destroy all these dirty things in due course of time. If we are faithful and wait patiently upon Him who is always faithful, we are sure to be successful.

What is the use of the honor or the power and the glory of this world? What will we gain from the pride we now take in this frail material body? False prestige and false pride are no more than empty dreams causing us to think that we are what we are not. After all, is it not useless to seek the pleasures of the flesh, which are so transitory but entail so much future suffering? Is it not foolish to hope for a long life on earth, and neglect our eternal life? We have only to seek the Kingdom of God first, and all material things will automatically follow.

Truly, the Kingdom of God is already at hand, and the Lord Himself is already present in the sound of His Holy Names.

☆☆☆☆☆☆☆☆☆☆☆☆☆☆☆☆☆☆

Meditation 2

Self-Knowledge With Humility

"IN THIS WORLD, there is nothing so sublime and pure as transcendental knowledge. Such knowledge is the mature fruit of all mysticism. And one who has achieved this enjoys the self within himself in due course of time." (*Bhagavad-gita* 4:38)

As much as it is natural to desire knowledge, it is important to desire the right kind. Knowledge in the hands of a fool is useless, if not downright dangerous. Modern science may have succeeded in splitting the atom and releasing almost immeasurable energy, but if that energy is used for destruction, what is its benefit? Even a child or an animal can destroy, but only God can create.

Lord Krishna advises us herein to seek transcendental knowledge, which benefits all and does not depend on any material condition. Indeed, a poor, illiterate devotee knows and satisfies the Lord far more completely than the greatest scientist or scholar who has no devotion.

Material education is not an end in itself but a means for understanding our eternal loving relationship with the Lord who made us. Instead of being puffed up with useless mundane learning and worldly abilities, we should cultivate real knowledge of the soul, for this will serve us well both now and hereafter.

Empty words and idle promises never satisfy anyone, what to speak of the soul; but a life of God consciousness leads to purity and peace of mind.

Krishna is pleased by the submissive humility of a devotee, not his erudition. After all, one who is truly intelligent knows that God is all in all, whereas a person who knows many things but does not know God knows nothing. "I am the Self seated in the hearts of all creatures," Lord Krishna declares. "I am the beginning, the middle and the end of all beings." (*Bg.* 10.20)

How can we feel proud of what is not even ours? Whatever ability we have comes from God. The very air we breathe, the things we possess, indeed, our body and soul are His. Therefore, as His stewards, we should dutifully use everything in His service and for His enjoyment.

In this light, the more talents we have, the greater our responsibility, and, conversely, the greater our condemnation if we misuse them. Sometimes immature devotees think that the best course of action is to negate all material influences and hide themselves in a secluded place. But this is like burning down your house because you can't pay the taxes. A more intelligent solution would be to make money with the house. Then there will be no difficulty in paying the taxes. Similarly, if we use all our talents in Krishna's service, we will never be put into difficulty due to material misuse, for the Lord promises to give us protection and to deliver us from all sinful reactions.

Of course, one who identifies with the material body and thinks in terms of "I and mine" is in the greatest ignorance. He can never find God or know himself as he is. As long as we feel even the slightest pride in ourselves, we are barred from His holy abode. Undoubtedly, the Lord is easily approached, but only by those who are materially exhausted. The path of material progress—aristocracy, opulence, education, and personal beauty—prevents us from devoutly calling upon His name.

Without the sincerity born of genuine humility, we cannot feelingly chant the Holy Name of the Lord. As a helpless child takes complete shelter of his parents, we must give ourselves up utterly to the Lord who has come in the form of His Holy Name. Then Lord Krishna, the swift deliverer of the defenseless, will surely come to our aid.

☆☆☆☆☆☆☆☆☆☆☆☆☆☆

Meditation 3

On Knowing The Truth

"ONLY UNTO THOSE great souls who simultaneously have implicit faith in both the Lord and the spiritual master are all the imports of Vedic knowledge automatically revealed." (*Svetasvatara Upanishad* 6.23)

Almost everyone says that he is searching for the Truth, and if one finds it, he is truly happy. But alas, since there are few happy faces in the world today, we must conclude that few have found it, and that what most call truth is but another lie. Real Truth is eternal, manifesting itself not in fads and fashions, nor in speculative opinions, but from the mouth of the Supreme Absolute Truth.

All our foolish discussions of mundane matters will not help us at the moment of death, for they are no more than mental creations, the products of imperfect senses. Though we have amassed a fortune and conquered the world, we cannot escape the Court of Yamaraj, lord of death, who judges all. Let us not neglect what is lasting and important in order to accomplish something of little or only temporal value.

The material body and mind are undoubtedly impermanent. Yet the world places all its concern in them, with no regard for the immortal soul. This is like nicely polishing a birdcage but never feeding the bird within. Just as the cage is useless without the bird, the body and mind have no meaning apart from the soul. Why, then, do men neglect the needs of the soul in their futile attempt to enjoy the perishable body?

These truths are understood by the meek and humble—even though they may be inexperienced or uneducated—but are hidden from the sophisticated, the philosophers, the professors and professional teachers. Sublime knowledge of the Almighty is automatically revealed to the pure in heart, to those who are free from the illusion of thinking, "I am great." God is great, and all others are small.

The desire to give up our own personal enjoyment for the service of the Lord is purified desire. Therefore, the humble devotee, following a life of plain living and high thinking, is not distracted by the glamorous attractions of this world. He acts only for the service of God and thereby finds peace and contentment. How can a man burdened with unfulfilled desires ever find peace?

For one who has learned to control his mind and senses, the art of surrender to the Lord and the spiritual master is both easy and natural. He learns to act through faith, not faith in his own imagination or inclination, but faith in the authority of Krishna and His representative, the bona fide spiritual master. By simple observation, we can understand that the way of private speculation is fraught with the danger of human defect.* Only a life of faith leads to transcendental knowledge.

Every material endeavor has some fault, and no man is learned in every sphere, but if we are guided by transcendental authorities, we will make no mistake. Our faith should be reasonable, intelligent, and effective. Why should we put faith in our senses, which are always imperfect? Perfection cannot be derived from imperfection, but only from perfection, just as a perfect mathematical answer cannot follow incorrect procedure. To have perfect knowledge, we must approach the perfect source—God Himself, or His representative, the pure devotee—

and follow in the authorized way.

If we took as much care to avoid sinful activity and the pitfalls to divine service as we do to solve the man-made problems of contemporary life, we would find fewer problems and less depravity, especially in our institutions of religious culture.

To become great means to serve the Great. The confidential servant of the king is almost on the level of the king. Serving the servant of God is the ideal of perfect God consciousness. One who seeks his own elevation is easily dragged down, but one who makes himself the servant of the servant becomes *prabhu*, master of the devotees.

⋆The four defects of conditioned souls are: 1) to commit mistakes; 2) to possess imperfect senses; 3) to be illusioned by the conception "I am this body"; and 4) to have a tendency to cheat.

☆☆☆☆☆☆☆☆☆☆☆☆☆☆☆

Meditation 4

The Symptoms Of A Holy Man

"THE SYMPTOMS OF a holy man are that he is tolerant, merciful, and friendly to all living entities. He has no enemies, he is peaceful, he abides by the scriptures, and all his characteristics are sublime." (*Srimad-Bhagavatam* 3:25:21)

Ordinary men generally give in to their senses and fail to consider carefully the ramifications of their actions. They follow neither intelligent reasoning nor wise counsel. But a saintly person, because he follows in the footsteps of the previous spiritual masters and is guided by the holy scriptures, exhibits all the godly qualities.

First and foremost among these is tolerance. It is easy to tolerate what we like from those we love, but what about tolerating the unlovely and the intolerable? Although the Lord often tests his devotee by subjecting him to very difficult and trying circumstances, a sincere devotee does not hesitate to perform his duty. Rather, he sees the challenge as the Lord's special mercy and a blessed chance to surrender to His will.

Furthermore, a devotee is very kind to others. Whereas he may be negligent of his own comforts and well-being, he always thinks of the welfare of others. In other words, he is self-sacrificing. Most of all, thinking of others' spiritual happiness, he wants to tell them about the Lord's merciful Holy Name, the greatest gift anyone can give or receive. Krishna has made Himself personally present in His Name, and we can find all satisfaction in its transcendental sound.

Because the devotee is friendly to all living entities, he does not willingly harm even an ant, nor inflict pain needlessly on anyone. Seeing the Supreme Lord within all beings, he treats each and every one as he himself would want to be treated. Therefore, when God has supplied us with such an abundance of beautiful and nutritious fruits, grains, vegetables, and milk, why slaughter innocent animals? We cannot expect to attain the divine vision that unites all creation in loving relationship to God when we are engaged in such bloody acts.

Moreover, a devotee has no enemies, and he is peaceful. A person with enemies engages in violence and becomes his own enemy by not knowing his real self-interest. How can he be peaceful? A devotee, however, treats all others as he would treat the Supreme Lord, the father of all. Always following the will of the Lord, he knows perfect peace.

In summary, it is said that all the characteristics of a devotee are sublime. This sublimity is not the impressiveness of worldly sophistication but the exalted glory that comes from plain living and high thinking. A pure life makes us sublime in Krishna's estimation and simultaneously gives us many other benefits. Most important, our pure life makes us more God conscious by making us humbler and more submissive to His will. Peace and wisdom are but by-products of a more intimate relationship with Him. By leading a life of blissful Krishna consciousness, the devotee becomes happy both in this life and the next.

☆☆☆☆☆☆☆☆☆☆☆☆☆☆☆

Meditation 5

Judging Transcendental Literatures

"THOSE WORDS WHICH do not describe the glories of the Lord, who alone can sanctify the atmosphere of the whole universe, are considered by saintly persons to be like unto a place of pilgrimage for crows. Since the all-perfect persons are inhabitants of the transcendental abode, they do not derive any pleasure there. On the other hand, that literature which is full of descriptions of the transcendental glories of the Name, fame, forms, pastimes, etc., of the unlimited Supreme Lord is a different creation, full of transcendental words directed toward bringing about a revolution in the impious lives of this world's misdirected civilization. Such transcendental literatures, even though imperfectly composed, are heard, sung and accepted by purified men who are thoroughly honest." (*Srimad-Bhagavatam* 1:5:10-11)

It is not eloquence that we seek in the holy books, but transcendental knowledge. If the books happen to be erudite and poetic, it is well and good, but we read for spiritual profit, not mental titillation.

In this regard, simple, devotional writings full of love for God are more prized by the devotee than the polished composition of a great scholar who lacks devotion. The above quotation compares such mundane literatures—however nicely decorated with metaphor and simile—to a place of pilgrimage for crows. We all know that crows gather in filthy places like rubbish heaps, where they relish decaying garbage. Similarly, materialists gather to read topics of mundane love and life, but such topics are rejected by enlightened men, who know very well that anything connected with the gross and subtle material body can at best bring temporary sense gratification, not satisfaction to the soul.

To be wise means to use our time wisely. A moment wasted can never be recalled, not even for millions of dollars. Therefore we should wisely cultivate a love for the simple and the pure. It is not wise to be swayed by a name, or an academic pedigree, or the looks of a person; rather, we should judge the truth of what is said. Two plus two equals four, no matter who says it, and whoever inspires us to love Krishna and forsake evil is our spiritual master and is worth hearing.

Let us listen submissively, then, to the saintly teachers, contemporary and ancient, who can present knowledge of the Absolute. Using our intelligence to inquire profoundly and humbly from them, let us show them due regard and have firm faith in their instruction. There is no use in challenging them impertinently or pretending to know what we don't. If we but seek Truth with an open mind and a pure heart, we shall surely find it.

☆☆☆☆☆☆☆☆☆☆☆☆☆☆☆

Meditation 6

Too Much Attachment

"IN THE MINDS of those who are too attached to sense enjoyment and material opulence, and who are bewildered by such things, the resolute determination of devotional service to the Supreme Lord does not take place." (*Bhagavad-gita* 2:44.)

Uncontrolled desire is never satisfied, and when we desire more than is necessary, we become entangled and enslaved by the object of our desire. Thus we become subjected to the kicks of material nature in the form of hankering and lamentation, which knock us back and forth like a football. At first we hanker for something, and then, when we are frustrated, we lament at not obtaining it, or we lament over its inevitable loss in due course of time. In any case, our peace of mind is disturbed. Furthermore, when we are proud and greedy, we are always in anxiety, for we try to assume the position of controller, despite being controlled by the Supreme Lord. But by living simply and thinking spiritually, we can remain pure in heart and always at rest.

A man who does not subdue his senses is easily tempted and often overcome by apparently insignificant sins. Being addicted to sense gratification, he lacks the spiritual strength that is a natural consequence of surmounting the trials and tribulations sent by the Lord. Because he is attached to the bodily conception of life and prone to over-indulgence in sensual pleasure, he can hardly fix his mind on the loving service of the Lord.

Indeed, a materialistic man becomes angry and blinded by passion when he is deprived of sense gratification. Ignorant of his own self-interest, he blasphemes the Lord and His devotees. A devotee, on the other hand, is trained to see everything as the loving mercy of Lord Krishna and as part of His all perfect plan. The devotee lives in peace and harmony now, and after this life, goes to the Kingdom of God; but the ungodly remain forever unhappy in the world of birth and death.

Real peace is found in resisting passion, and lasting happiness is attained by engaging our senses in the service of the Lord. Our senses cry out for positive fulfillment, which cannot be found by remaining inactive or void. Bliss and contentment are experienced in serving Hrisikesa, the Master of the senses. We can perfectly serve by hearing about Him, chanting His glories, remembering His pastimes, worshiping the Deity in the temple, personally serving the Lord, carrying out His orders, acting as the Lord's friend, and surrendering everything to Him. The senses become perfect when one performs even one of these items, what to speak of two or more. But the easiest and most sublime method of all, especially recommended for this age, is the chanting of the Hare Krishna maha-mantra: Hare Krishna, Hare Krishna, Krishna Krishna, Hare Hare; Hare Rama, Hare Rama, Rama Rama, Hare Hare. Chant and be happy!

☆☆☆☆☆☆☆☆☆☆☆☆☆☆☆☆☆

Meditation 7

Thinking Oneself Lowly

"ONE SHOULD CHANT the Holy Name of the Lord in a humble state of mind, thinking oneself lower than the straw in the street; one should be more tolerant than a tree, devoid of all sense of false prestige, and should be ready to offer all respect to others. In such a state of mind one can chant the Holy Name of the Lord constantly." (*Sikshastaka*, 3.)

Real religion is more than executing formulas or performing rituals. Man looks on the outward appearance, but God sees the heart. Even if we are chanting the Holy Name—truly the best of all activities—we will fail to please the Lord unless our heart has become soft with compassion and cleansed of the tendency to criticize others.

Why are we ashamed to serve others, wanting instead to be treated as superior? Do we not know that everyone's heart is the abode of Lord Krishna? We may possess some valuable talent, but to God, our material qualifications are no more than filthy rags. It is far more important what He thinks of us than what our neighbor thinks, or even what we think of ourselves.

Nor should we take much pleasure in the condition of the body; that which is born soon grows old and dies, no matter how attractive and beautiful it may be. Great material assets—education, wealth, fame, or power—soon pass into oblivion. Foolish is the person who seeks the things of this world and puts his trust in them.

If God has given us wealth, it is well and good, but we must use it for Him, not for sense gratification. Sense indulgence acts just like poison: however sweet the taste, the end is death. If we have friends, well and good; let's show ourselves friendly by teaching them Krishna consciousness.

We should not depend on men, but on the Almighty. We should not boast of our talents and abilities, but give credit to God, who is the ability in man and the rightful owner of all that be. Then we will not become thieves by falsely claiming God's property as our own, nor be punished by His laws of nature in this life and the next.

Lord Chaitanya admonishes us to be humble like straw in the street and tolerant like a tree. Even if we walk on straw and trample it under-foot, it does not protest, and a tree is so kind that it gives its shade, fruit, branches, even its very life, without protest. Being completely devoid of all sense of false prestige, we must learn to see the good in others and the faults in ourselves. We should never think ourselves superior, lest God Himself declare us inferior. When one tries to elevate himself, he makes himself mean; but whoever makes himself lowly is exalted by the Most Exalted. The humble are dear to the Lord, and the Lord is dear to them, but those who are proud and envious live in hell, in fear, and in anger. Humility attracts Krishna, and those who chant His Holy Name in a humble state of mind find unending joy and peace.

☆☆☆☆☆☆☆☆☆☆☆☆☆☆☆☆

Meditation 8

Symptoms Of Love

"THE SIX SYMPTOMS of love shared by one devotee and another are: offering gifts in charity, accepting charitable gifts, revealing one's mind in confidence, inquiring confidentially, accepting _prasada_, and offering _prasada_." (_Nectar of Instruction_, Text Four.)

Mr. Worldly Wise cautions us not to open our hearts or reveal our innermost thoughts, lest others take advantage of us, but here Rupa Goswami specifically advises us to relish the exchange of confidences. Of course, knowing themselves to be spirit souls, not material bodies, devotees are transcendental to the bodily conception of life. As such, they are not subject to the envy that characterizes the dealings of those who identify themselves with the gross or subtle body. Indeed, on the spiritual level there is no question of "yours" or "mine," for in reality, everything belongs to God. Devotees therefore relish the privilege of giving in charity to please Lord Krishna and thus receive His mercy. This is called Krishna consciousness.

Seeing all living beings as parts and parcels of the Lord, a devotee does not judge others by external appearance. He does not shun the elderly, thinking them a botheration; he does not avoid the young, disdaining their frivolity. He does not turn away the strangers within his gate out of fear that they may cheat him. He does not court the rich, nor deride the poor, nor seek favors from the aristocratic and powerful, nor allow himself to be swayed by the so-called learned. He is intimate only with his lawful wife and sees all other women as his mother. He is free from the passion for honor and the desire for personal gratification. In short, a devotee is happy if he can associate with other devotees of kindred hearts, who are humble in spirit, virtuous in action, free from the tendency to gossip and criticize, and above all, pure in their love for God.

Being full of love for others, a devotee wants to share with others. *Prasadam* means "the Lord's mercy," and devotees take great pleasure in giving and receiving this special mercy that comes in the form of food. *Prasadam* is not ordinary nourishment, for it provides sustenance for both the body and soul. Moreover, it is cooked with love and devotion for Krishna, the original giver of all. Because *prasadam* is offered to Krishna before anyone else, a devotee is concerned to cook cleanly and carefully for Krishna's pleasure. This meditation is the perfection of yoga. Not only in preparation, but also in eating, the devotee remains conscious that *prasadam* is special. Because Krishna has actually eaten it in His spiritual way and left us the remnants for our bodily maintenance, a sincere devotee relishes a special taste due to the touch of Krishna's lips. This may seem fantastic to the nonbeliever, but it is an everyday experience for the devotee.

Still, our charity will be incomplete and our loving experience unfulfilled if we do not give our friends and acquaintances the greatest gift of all: the Holy Name of the Lord. By chanting and inducing others to chant, we become the most munificent welfare workers. This mission, of course, is not our concoction, but the causeless mercy of Lord Chaitanya Mahaprabhu, the incarnation who appeared in India only five hundred years ago to teach this sublime process of chanting God's Holy Names. By His divine grace, we can also act as humble instruments and distribute His mercy to all. All glories to Lord Chaitanya, the Savior of all who call on His Name!

☆☆☆☆☆☆☆☆☆☆☆☆☆☆

Meditation 9

Submission

"JUST TRY TO learn the truth by approaching a spiritual master. Inquire from him submissively and render service unto him. The self-realized soul can impart knowledge unto you because he has seen the truth." (*Bhagavad-gita* 4.34)

Religion calling for submission, obedience, and surrender is not very fashionable in contemporary society. The purveyors of modern relativistic morality decry it as "brainwashing," and "slave mentality," or "the opiate of the masses." Lest he be thought a tyrant, one dares not speak of a wife being submissive to her husband, or a child being obedient to his parents. Yet it is a very wonderful thing to learn to obey, to have a benevolent and loving superior to whom we can dedicate our life. Indeed, it is far safer to carry out an order than to command.

Unfortunately, many people obey only due to force of circumstance or from lack of understanding, rather than out of love. For them, discontent and rejection occur at the least provocation. But if we can surrender to a truly bona fide spiritual master, who is the earthly representative of God, we are most fortunate, and we should be willing and enthusiastic in our service. Peace of mind and satisfaction of the soul very soon follow.

Even in this material world, peace and prosperity flourish where there is wholehearted submission to benevolent authority. A state plagued with rebellious citizens cannot prosper, and idle promises of utopia resulting from some whimsical, speculative change of party or philosophy are merely for the delusion of the masses. It is natural for the soul to want unlimited freedom to do whatever he pleases because we are by nature free, but such unrestricted liberty is not possible in a sinful world. Indeed, it is promised only by those who would cheat us of what freedom we have. In the spiritual world, however, we do have almost unlimited freedom, because liberty never becomes license there. Although our desire for freedom is natural, we are now in a diseased condition because we have chosen a life of selfish gratification. We have misused our original independence, which is given to us to render service to God. Until we learn submission to God's will, there will be no remission of the material disease, nor any decline in its debilitating effects. Real freedom is the freedom to love, and the freedom to love is the freedom to serve.

We should never think very highly of ourselves. After all, our opinions are always subject to the four defects of conditioned souls: imperfect senses, a tendency to make mistakes, illusion due to identification with the material body, and a cheating propensity. Therefore, it is imperative to become an attentive hearer of the Lord and His representatives, who are free from these defects.

Furthermore, even though we may have valid and useful ideas for serving Him, He is actually more pleased when—for the sake of peace and harmony—we simply accept those bona fide authorities whom He has placed over us. It has often been said that being a good hearer is a thousand times better than being a good speaker, and far safer besides. Unwillingness to hear from others even though they be empowered by God is a sign of false pride and obstinacy, which are productive of neither peace nor truth. If we learn to be a faithful hearer, we will surely become a faithful follower. Our love of God will not be measured by how loudly we proclaim that love, but how we execute His order.

☆☆☆☆☆☆☆☆☆☆☆☆☆☆

Meditation 10

Controlling The Urge To Speak

"A SOBER PERSON who can tolerate the urge to speak, the mind's demands, the actions of anger and the urges of the tongue, belly and genitals is qualified to make disciples all over the world." (*Nectar of Instruction*, text one.)

Of the six pushings or urges that keep one from being fixed in Krishna consciousness, the urge to speak is at the top of the list. To avoid this danger, impersonalist yogis and ascetics sometimes take vows of silence, but this is not the real message of this verse. Lord Jesus Christ pointed out that from the same mouth come both blessings and curses. It is not the power of speech in itself that is good or bad, but how words are used. The problem is not in the mouth, but in the heart. Repeating the words of God or His pure devotee is indeed the very means of conquering the unbridled senses and purifying the heart, but indulging in mundane talks and idle gossip leads to hell. Idle gossip, rumor mongering, and discussions of useless worldly topics—even if done innocently—greatly distract us from Krishna consciousness. They sap our enthusiasm for devotional service. They do not edify us, but quickly ensnare us in the illusory energy, *maya*.

How often we wish that we had held our peace or had not associated with that materialistic person! The urge to speak unnecessarily is almost irresistible, but seldom do we indulge without suffering a troubled conscience or an agitated mind. We indulge this urge only because we seek shelter in the false enjoyment of mundane conversation, wishing to divert the thoughts of the uncontrolled and flickering mind. Therefore we speak and joke of things we find very pleasurable or even those we intensely abhor. In either case, idle words serve no good purpose and do not tend toward enlightenment. Therefore, we must always be on guard to engage the restless tongue in chanting the Holy Name of the Lord or in speaking about His transcendental pastimes. A moment wasted is gone forever.

When the proper time comes, we should speak something positive and devotional. This is for the welfare of all. The Holy Bible advises us, "Let thy speech be short, comprehending much in few words." (*Ecclesiasticus* 32.8)

Of course, if we always speak about Krishna, we can speak unlimitedly, for He is transcendental, above the modes of material nature, and His qualities and pastimes are unlimited.

But as long as we have a material body, there remains the chance of misusing our tongue. Bad habits, inattention, and indifference to the life of the spirit make us lose control of the tongue. We must cultivate a new habit: using the tongue only to converse about the Lord and His service. But cultivation implies hard work; therefore, one who is serious about making progress must apply himself diligently to the task of hearing, conversing about, and chanting the Holy Name of the Lord constantly. This remedy is always effective.

☆☆☆☆☆☆☆☆☆☆☆☆☆☆☆☆☆

Meditation 11

Attaining Peace By Spiritual Quest

"A PERSON WHO is not disturbed by the incessant flow of desires—that enter like rivers into the ocean, which is ever being filled but is always still—can alone achieve peace, and not the man who strives to satisfy such desires. A person who has given up all desires for sense gratification, who lives free from desires, who has given up all sense of proprietorship, and is devoid of false ego—he alone can attain real peace. That is the way of the spiritual and godly life, after attaining which a man is not bewildered. Being so situated, even at the hour of death, one can enter into the Kingdom of God." (*Bhagavad-gita* 2:70-72)

If we want peace, we must learn to avoid the cause of disturbance. But it is a fact that what is soothing to one person is irritating to another. Thus, to become a fit candidate for peace, we must control the mind and senses because then we cannot be disturbed even when there is cause, whereas a man who does not practice such control would be disturbed even in paradise.

There are many practical suggestions for developing self-control, and these can also help us attain peace of mind. We will be greatly relieved by not caring about the foolish criticism of others and not meddling in the affairs of those who are not our charges. By avoiding duplicity and always dealing in an honest, straightforward manner, we can progress toward tranquility. Great peace and contentment come to him who neither listens to tales of the shortcomings and faults of others, nor repeats them, nor sits in judgement over the deeds of others, remembering that it is God Himself who judgeth every man.

It is beneficial for us to look to the great devotees of bygone days and learn from them the secret of godly living. Krishna advises us to learn from the ancients, and *Srimad-Bhagavatam* instructs us to follow the path of the *Mahajans,* the great authorities of Krishna consciousness. Unfortunately, being preoccupied with our own materialistic speculations and mental conceptions and consequently attached to the ephemeral things of this world, we are slow to take up the fight against *maya* and conquer even one vice. If only we could realize the great opportunity this human life affords, we would be driven with unbreakable determination to improve ourselves day by day.

Instead, our faith remains lukewarm, and we lack enthusiasm for the things of the spirit. If we would but seriously undergo the process of penance and austerity, controlling the body and mind, we would awaken our dormant Krishna consciousness and develop a taste for hearing about God. We would then experience something of the bliss that is our true nature.

There are three gates leading to hell: lust, anger, and greed. Without conquering them, we cannot be peaceful. For the conditioned soul to do this alone is certainly very difficult, but with the help of God, even the most difficult tasks become easy. Significantly, these hellish gates are first opened by contemplation. As soon as we think about sense objects, we become attached to them, and then lust and anger develop. We must stop desiring sense gratification and become resolute in our determination to use this life only for devotional service. As soon as there is a slight obstacle, we become dejected and give up the fight. If we would only try to stand firm in the fight and depend on the help and mercy of Krishna, we would surely emerge victorious. Indeed, the Lord promises, "My devotee will never perish."

If we would overcome just one sinful habit each year, we would soon be sinless. Sad to say, each year we often become a little more lax in our devotional life, until only a faint glimmer of our original enthusiasm remains. This ought not to be. We must counteract this tendency by always pressing forward with renewed vigor to become master of the senses. How else will we realize the sublime truth of being spirit soul, part and parcel of God? Unless we give up attachment for temporal pleasures, how will we ever know pleasures that are eternal?

By always practicing the regulative principles of freedom, we can attain lasting peace. It is simply a matter of practice. If we resist temptations at the beginning, we will never have a bad habit to break. By beginning with small things, we can progress to the more difficult. We should depend on the mercy of the *guru* and Krishna, and out of their causeless mercy, they will give us the light to find our way back home, back to Godhead.

☆☆☆☆☆☆☆☆☆☆☆☆☆☆

Meditation 12

The Value Of Hardships And Austerity

"I WISH THAT all those calamities would happen again and again so that we can see You again and again, for seeing You means that we will no longer see repeated births and deaths. My dear Lord, Your Lordship can easily be approached, but only by those who are materially exhausted. One who is on the path of material progress, trying to improve himself with respectable parentage, great opulence, high education and bodily beauty, cannot approach You with sincere feeling." (*Srimad-Bhagavatam* 1:8:25-26)

Generally we consider ourselves blessed if life goes smoothly and according to our desires. But sometimes it is better for us when it doesn't. Trials and tribulations are often very purifying, for in difficult times a devotee, having no other shelter, thinks of the Lord with greater intensity. It is easy then to become aware of our dangerous position in this material world. As the scriptures inform us, there is danger at every step; indeed, death itself is always staring us in the face. Nevertheless, in times of material well-being, we tend to forget this and try to make arrangements for permanent happiness here, even though all material attempts are doomed to frustration.

Therefore, it is sometimes good to suffer reverses, to be misjudged by men, and even apparently neglected by God. These difficulties are meant to help us in our progressive march toward Krishna consciousness. Our great fear should be not of bodily discomfort, but of pride, the plague of the soul. Especially dangerous is the unseemly spiritual pride that often comes to the neophyte, for this is an abomination to God. Adversity helps us to be humble and protects us from vainglory. One who has firmly rooted himself in pure love of Krishna can never be agitated, even in the most disturbing circumstances. Men may praise him or blame him; it does not matter, for the Lord knows the heart of His devotee, and the devotee knows the heart of his Lord.

The greatest test, however, comes when a devotee, sincerely trying to do what is right, is afflicted with evil thoughts and passions. Before them, he often feels helpless and alone. This is the dark night of the soul; yet, one in knowledge knows that he is never alone. The Almighty is everywhere, and especially with His devotee. Krishna specifically promises, "I will give you all protection." In the hour of greatest need, the devotee must remember the words of his Lord, place his hand in

His, and cry out, "Lead on, my Lord, lead on."

In our distress, though weakened by misery and suffering, we should call out to Him who always hears, and pray for His merciful deliverance. Then we are sure to be successful. When we cannot bear His separation any longer, when we are fully wearied of living apart from Him, then He, our Savior from birth and death, will give us His protection. He has made Himself easily available in the sound of His Holy Name.

☆☆☆☆☆☆☆☆☆☆☆☆☆☆☆☆

Meditation 13

The Secret Of Resisting Temptation

"WHILE CONTEMPLATING THE objects of the senses, a person develops attachment for them, and from such attachment lust develops, and from lust, anger arises. From anger, delusion arises, and from delusion, bewilderment of memory. When memory is bewildered, intelligence is lost, and when intelligence is lost, one falls down again into the material pool." (*Bhagavad-gita* 2:62-63)

Because we have taken birth in the material world due to material desires, we are again and again subjected to various temptations and allurements. On the Battlefield of Kurukshetra, Arjuna asked Krishna what compels a man to commit sin even though he may not want to. The Supreme Lord replied, "It is lust only, Arjuna...which is the all-devouring, sinful enemy of this world." (*Bg.* 3.38)

What is this lust, and where does it come from? Is it from the devil, from some evil being? If so, what is his origin? If we say that everything comes from God, does that make God evil? That cannot be! By definition He is all good, and therefore, whatever He does is good. Even if He exhibits the quality that we call lust, that quality is not bad in Him. In fact, it is the highest good, for this world is like a reflection, and what is highest in reality is lowest in the reflection, and what is highest in the reflection, is lowest in reality. In Him, that which we call lust is perfect love.

What then is the difference between love and lust? To love means to repose one's affections entirely in one person, without being diverted to any other, under any condition, and without the slightest desire for personal gratification. God is one and self-contained. Nothing exists apart from Him. Therefore He is perfect love. But because we have separated ourselves from Him by forgetfulness of our intimate relationship, we sometimes place our affections in others. Thus, our original love for Krishna has become spoiled and perverted into a love for temporary material objects. This perverted love is more properly called lust.

Seen in this way, every temptation is but a prostitute coming to steal away our love from its natural object, Lord Krishna. Whether it be the urge to speak nonsense, engage in frivolity, waste time reading mundane literatures, watch idiotic television shows and movies, amass money, or engage in illicit sexual affairs, we are being seduced by false lovers.

Thus, we must ever be on guard to resist temptations, lest *maya* capture us by lust and destroy our real love—love of God. Moreover, we are warned in this verse to resist such temptations from the very beginning, before they take hold, by not even thinking about them. Every evil deed begins with an evil thought. If we do not even contemplate sense gratification, *maya* will have no chance to delude us. No one in this world is so holy and perfect that he is not sometimes tested by Krishna, and no one is so weak that Krishna cannot give him strength to resist.

Temptation is a test. If we fail the test, we fall from divine grace and become further estranged from the Lord. But the opposite is also true. If we pass His test, we become stronger and come closer to Him. Therefore, the dealings of God are always good, though apparently troublesome and severe. Not only do they humble and correct us, but they purify and strengthen us by forcing us to take complete shelter of Him.

Just as we fall down by contemplating the objects of the senses, we become victorious by contemplating the things of the spirit. Simply by uttering the Name of Krishna, or thinking of His pastimes, we receive the complete protection of the Lord, for there is no difference between the Lord and His Name, or the Lord and remembrance of Him.

Some devotees face great temptations in the beginning of their spiritual lives, while others must face them later on. Others, again, seem to face little or no difficulty. Those who do not know the science of Krishna consciousness and the laws of *karma* find this hard to understand, but we should rest assured that everything is happening according to the infinite plan of the Almighty, and for the ultimate good of His devotees.

Neophyte devotees often try to escape difficulties and tests of surrender by running away, changing their duties, or seeking consolation in old friends, only to find themselves further removed from the Lord's mercy and more deeply ensnared by illusion. We cannot defeat the enemy simply by running or changing our material circumstances. But we can become stronger than our enemy by faith in God, proved by our patience and true humility. The urges for sense gratification must be uprooted completely, not only partially and superficially, lest, like a cut-off weed, they return with renewed vigor.

By perseverence and firm faith in God we are guaranteed to make progress toward our goal. After all, God helps all surrendered souls. Let us learn to take counsel from those devotees who are more devout, and try to help others who may be weak in faith by our example and our testimony to the bliss and perfection of Krishna consciousness. Let no man despair: the all-loving God never tempts us beyond our capacity to resist. Therefore, let us be humble and grateful to the Lord in the face of temptation, remembering that He has promised to protect and honor His devotee who is faithful to the end.

It has been said that temptations and trials measure the progress of our life. In them, advancement and virtue become manifest. As fire purifies gold, temptation purifies a devotee. One who is never tested has no difficulty appearing fervent and devout, but one who can tolerate and·overcome adversity makes great progress. Let us always guard against temptation by taking shelter of the Lord's special mercy in the form of His Holy Name. He will never fail us.

☆☆☆☆☆☆☆☆☆☆☆☆☆☆

Meditation 14

The Mad Elephant Offense

"THE CHARACTERISTIC OF Ramachandra Puri was that first he would induce someone to eat more than necessary and then he would criticize him.

"One who is attached to dry speculative knowledge has no relationship with Krishna. His occupation is criticizing Vaishnavas. Thus he is situated in criticism." (*Chaitanya Charitamrita*, Antya 8:17, 27)

"Judge not that ye be not judged" is some of the best advice ever given. To unnecessarily criticize others is a great disqualification in spiritual life. Unable to give up this habit, Ramachandra Puri criticized even his spiritual master, Madhavendra Puri, and the Supreme Personality of Godhead, Lord Sri Chaitanya. Such an offense has been likened to a mad elephant entering a garden. Just as a garden can be devastated by the trampling of an elephant, spiritual life can be undone by the tendency to criticize others.

Indeed, the first offense against the Holy Name is to blaspheme or criticize pure devotees who have dedicated their lives to the propagation of Krishna consciousness. Being the greatest manifestation of mercy, the Holy Names of the Lord can counter the effects of all kinds of sinful activities, but if one is critical of pure devotees, his chanting will have no effect.

Therefore, it is better to turn our attention to ourselves, judging ourselves ever so severely, and beware of maliciously criticizing even the least of the Lord's devotees. Being very partial to His devotees, Krishna never tolerates even a slight offense at the feet of a surrendered soul.

What do we ultimately gain by criticizing others? It is a useless affair, often mistaken in fact and frequently harmful in effect. We often see things as we would like them to be, but because our perspective is tainted with selfish interest, we cannot judge aright. We should remember that, in God's service, someone with a different opinion may be just as sincere and correct as we are. The Lord respects his opinion as much as ours. The real point is to see that Krishna is always in the center, for this makes everything perfect.

Even the Lord's most intimate associates, the *gopis* of Vrindaban, disagree over how best to serve the Lord. Indeed, Krishna relishes such disagreement. We are not impersonalists; we know that we are all individual parts and parcels of the Lord. Therefore each of us can serve the Lord in his own unique way, just as if we were each His only begotten son.

God is moved not by external appearance, but by genuine affection. We need to rely less on our own intelligence and hard endeavor and more upon the beauty of submission and surrender. Humility, tolerance, and ardent love are far more attractive to Krishna than human wisdom multiplied a million times.

✮✮✮✮✮✮✮✮✮✮✮✮✮✮✮✮✮

Meditation 15

True Charity—Equality Of Vision

"THE HUMBLE SAGE, by virtue of true knowledge, sees with equal vision a learned and gentle *brahmana*, a cow, an elephant, a dog and a dog-eater." (*Bhagavad-gita* 5:18)

According to *Bhagavad-gita*, charity can be performed either in goodness, passion, or ignorance. A gift given to a worthy person, at the proper time and place, out of duty rather than with the expectation of return, is charity in the mode of goodness. Something done grudgingly, or with a desire for benefit, is charity in the mode of passion. But charity that neglects the rules and regulations and is unbeneficial to others is in the mode of darkness. Still, none of these are real charity.

Real charity is more than business, or even duty. It comes from the heart and goes to the heart. It is rooted in love of God, with the understanding that everything is meant for His satisfaction. He is the Supreme Enjoyer of all that be, nothing excluded. Therefore, real charity begins with absolute, universal vision.

That does not mean, however, that real charity is akin to dry, speculative knowledge. The essence of charity is Love of God, which is all-encompassing, just as the Lord Himself is. Jesus Christ said that the first and great commandment—to love God with the whole heart—cannot be separated from the second: to love one's neighbor as oneself. And who is our neighbor? The humble sage sees every living being as his neighbor, for Lord Krishna clearly says, "I am the seed-giving Father of all living entities." This makes everyone our brother.

How then can we slaughter innocent animals just because we like the taste of their flesh? They are also God's sons, our brothers and neighbors. "Do unto others as you would have them do unto you" applies to even the most insignificant creature in the Kingdom of God.

It is this universal vision that makes for real charity. Mundane philanthrophy is of little value, but charity performed according to spiritual vision pleases the Lord, who regards more the love of the devotee than the object that is given.

Love is so transcendentally satisfying that even a leaf, a flower, a piece of fruit or some water satisfies God when offered with love. But without this love, whatever greatness we possess—fame, fortune, talent, mystic powers—is no more valuable than counterfeit money or fool's gold. Even transcendental knowledge and the ability to speak eloquently on spiritual topics by citing all the revealed scriptures are dry and lifeless accomplishments without love. Giving away all our possessions and practicing all kinds of severe austerities and penances can only harden the heart if not done with love.

This perfect love manifests all good qualities. Above all, it is merciful and kind; it is humbler than a blade of grass, and therefore faultless and true. Without seeking material possessions for itself, it is magnanimous and equal to all. Being personally mild and clean, perfect love works tirelessly for the welfare of everyone.

Because a devotee has no desire for self satisfaction, he is peaceful. Because he is always surrendered to Krishna, material affections cannot disturb him. He is completely fixed in His service and free from all bad habits. He eats only as much as required and is sane and sober. Respectful toward others, without false prestige, grave and compassionate, he is a friend to all. Being perfect in love, he is always poetic, expert, and silent.

Beware of imitation. There is that which professes to be charity or love, but is, in fact, sensuality. Our own inclinations and desires for reward and recognition are motives that frequently taint our deeds. But one who would be perfect in his sacrifice must seek nothing for himself. He must act only for the glory and satisfaction of the Almighty. This is easily accomplished if we have the guidance of a true spiritual master, the representative of God. He guides us from without, while the Lord Himself guides from within. We can be free from the enemies of haughtiness and jealousy when we see that it is He who does all things according to His own perfect will.

Truly, if we have but the smallest measure of real charity, we can become detached from all the glitter of this world and gradually develop pure love for Krishna, the real goal of life.

☆☆☆☆☆☆☆☆☆☆☆☆☆☆☆

Meditation 16

A Devotee Is Perfect

"ALL THE DEMIGODS and their exalted qualities, such as religion, knowledge, and renunciation, become manifest in the body of one who has developed unalloyed devotion for the Supreme Personality of Godhead, Vasudeva. On the other hand, a person devoid of devotional service and engaged in material activities has no good qualities. Even if he is adept at the practice of mystic yoga, or the honest endeavor of maintaining his family and relatives, he must be driven by his own mental speculations and must engage in the service of the Lord's external energy. How can there be any good qualities in such a man?" (*Srimad-Bhagavatam* 5:18:12)

Being a perfect devotee does not mean that one has no material faults, but that such faults are insignificant in the light of unalloyed devotion. Although the full moon may be marred with a few dark spots, its brilliance can light our way in the darkness of night. Only a fool would criticize the moon for its spots, and only a fool, or a man who is as envious as a snake or demon, will decry the Lord's devotee for some temporary deviation. Indeed, Krishna Himself declares in *Bhagavadgita* that His devotee is always to be considered saintly, despite possible discrepancies in social behavior. Such is the force of pure devotional service.

What is that special quality of devotional service so pleasing to Krishna that He overlooks everything else? What is the special sweetness of that love that makes the Lord Himself hanker for the association of His devotee? It is not personal beauty, nor material expertise, nor even the attainment of transcendental knowledge. Unalloyed love is characterized by the absence of all material hankerings, and the unalloyed devotee completely abandons himself to the shelter of his Lord. He does not think that he has anything to offer the Lord, nor does he demand anything in return. Rather, he prays only to be engaged in the transcendental loving service of his Lord.

Such a pure devotee never thinks highly of himself, although he is most exalted. Krishnadas Kaviraja, the author of *Chaitanya Charitamrita*, used to say, "I am so sinful that if you simply remember my name, you will lose all your pious credits." He not only said this, but he actually felt this way. Although he considered himself completely unworthy, he was a most elevated devotee because he was fully surrendered to Lord Chaitanya. Full surrender means having no other hope, no other shelter, and no other resting place for the mind and senses than Krishna. The *gopis* of Vrindaban are the greatest example of surrendered souls because they allowed Krishna to do whatever He wished to them. They abandoned their homes, friends, husbands, children. They were willing to sacrifice religious principles, and even life itself for the satisfaction of Krishna. This is why the Lord told them, "It is impossible to repay you for your love; therefore, please be satisfied by your own pious activities."

It is also true that earlier, when those same *gopis* felt a little proud of their unique position, Krishna disappeared from their sight. If, by miscalculation, a devotee becomes puffed up in his service, the Lord withdraws Himself. Then the devotee, being humbled and feeling lost and lifeless without his Lord, again seeks shelter at His Lotus Feet. Just as a helpless child cries for his mother, the unalloyed devotee cries for Krishna in despair. Tears of love are the only price for obtaining Him.

Meditation 17

The Value Of Spiritual Retreats

"HOW WONDERFUL IT is that simply by residing in Mathura even for one day, one can achieve a transcendental loving attitude toward the Supreme Personality of Godhead! This land of Mathura must be more glorious than Vaikunthadhama, the Kingdom of God." (*Padma Purana*)

If we want peace and contentment, we should go where they are easily available. Gold is not to be found in a refuse heap, nor peace in the rat race of material endeavor. A transcendental place where the Lord exhibited His earthly pastimes, or where these pastimes are heard and sung by pure devotees, is the right place to seek relief from the distress of material life. Living in a spiritual community in the association of advanced devotees is one of the five most important items recommended by Srila Rupa Goswami for rapid progress in Krishna consciousness. To remain in such a place may not always be easy, but those who do so, strictly observing the devotional process, are guaranteed to go back home, back to Godhead.

One who lives in a *dhama*, or holy place, should always think of himself as an exile from the material world. And he should meditate on his good fortune in being able to stay in a little sample of the spiritual world kindly provided by the mercy of Krishna. In this way, he will remain content with whatever bodily necessities are provided, preferring to concentrate more on the culture of the spirit than on the comfort of the body. After all, whatever luxuries we gain for the body are lost at death, but even the smallest spiritual gain benefits us eternally.

Therefore, if we are serious in our devotional life, we will forsake our worldly standards and ambitions. We may be considered fools by the so-called wise men of this world, but the satisfaction of God should be more important to us than the praise of men. Society may be impressed by a sophisticated and economically advanced civilization, but the Lord is attracted only by the pure in heart and humble in spirit. Today, unfortunately, such pure and humble persons are rarely found.

If we seek anything other than God and loving service to His Lotus Feet, we are sure to find only frustration and grief. If we cannot humble ourselves by becoming "servant of the servant" for His sake, then we cannot attain peace in this world or the next.

We should constantly remember that our position is not to rule, but to serve. We have fallen into this world due to our desire to lord it over God's creation, and this is the cause of our continued material bondage. As long as this disease of unlawful desire remains, we will be forced to stay here and undergo repeated birth and death. We must learn to serve, to suffer, and to work for Krishna. We being eternal servants of God, that is our constitutional nature. Even in this world, people suffer and work very hard, but they do so for personal sense gratification. But if we act for Krishna's satisfaction, all problems will be solved. If we work in this way, shunning idle gossip, not wasting time, and avoiding all forms of sinful activity, the whole world can prosper forever. If we don't, our purpose is lost, and our efforts are as useless as a broken water pot or a severed hand. A holy place of pilgrimage acts just like a refiner's fire: it purifies whatever is put into it. Only those who have no desire for spirituality are untouched.

☆☆☆☆☆☆☆☆☆☆☆☆☆☆☆☆☆☆

Meditation 18

Following In The Footsteps

"ALL THE LIBERATED souls in ancient times acted with this understanding [renouncing the fruits of action] and so attained liberation. Therefore, as the ancients, you should perform your duty in this divine consciousness." (*Bhagavad-gita* 4:15)

When we are young and immature, we dream of making a new world, pioneering lands yet unexplored, or rebelling for the sake of rebelling. But when we grow older, we find that we do not know it all, that our ability to comprehend is indeed quite limited, and that perhaps the best course of action is to follow in the footsteps of a worthy predecessor. In this regard, Lord Krishna advises that since our senses are imperfect and limited, and the Absolute Truth is perfect and unlimited, our only chance for perfection lies in following the transcendental path of the *Mahajans*, the great saints of Krishna consciousness.

Indeed, our lives seem puny in comparison to theirs. Many performed austerities unimaginable today. Dhruva Maharaj, for example, began his penances by eating only dry leaves and berries, and finally he even stopped breathing. As recently as five hundred years ago, Raghunath Das Goswami ate only the grains left uneaten by the cows in Jagannath Puri. Others, like Prahlad Maharaj, suffered at the hands of cruel demons: Hiranyakasipu tried to kill young Prahlad in many ways—by poisoning him, by crushing him with huge stones, by throwing him into a pit of venomous snakes, and by boiling him in oil—but he could not, for Prahlad was protected by the Supreme Personality of Godhead. Even Lord Krishna's personal friends, the Pandavas, were harassed and endangered by the envious Duryodhana and his followers, but ultimately Krishna saved them. Again and again, Krishna confirms His promise: "My devotee will never perish."

Others, like Sanatan and Rupa Goswami, renounced great earthly positions, riches, honor, and aristocratic society for the sake of serving Lord Chaitanya. They have shown us that the treasures of this world are to be considered rubbish in the street. Not only were such devotees not attracted to opulence, but they hardly allowed themselves life's necessities. Always absorbed in ecstatic love of Krishna, they considered mundane pleasure demeaning to the soul. Although they were poor in the things of this world, they were rich in spiritual treasures: love, joy, peace, virtue, and unlimited mercy. Outwardly they were beggars; inwardly they were full of divine grace and transcendental vision.

Similarly, our beloved spiritual master, Srila Prabhupada, provided us with a most wonderful example of Krishna consciousness. Even at the advanced age of seventy, he did not hesitate to leave the serenity and transcendental pleasure of Vrindaban in order to bring Lord Chaitanya's mercy to the most fallen people of the western world. Traveling alone and without support, he depended solely on the protection of Krishna. Enduring all kinds of hardships, neglected and criticized by his Godbrothers, and not caring for worldly praise, he proved himself to be most honored and beloved by Krishna. Showing true humility and absolute obedience to the order of his spiritual master, he kindly pointed the way home, back to Godhead.

Such great souls should be our example and inspiration. Their influence on our lives ought always to shine brightly, for they can bring us to the highest perfection of life: unalloyed love of Krishna. This will also protect us from the dimming influence of those who are weak of faith and lukewarm in enthusiasm.

If we can remember the great devotion, complete dedication, and unbreakable determination of the great souls, we will certainly progress toward our transcendental goal, even through periods of great testing. How absorbed these great souls were in hearing and chanting the Name and fame of the Lord! How perfect their lives, so full of virtue and renunciation! Pure love of God was manifest through perfect obedience to their spiritual masters. Their footprints are still fresh and clear, urging us on to perfection. Truly, these great souls, holy and perfect in every way, have defeated *maya's* illusion and opened wide the doors of that transcendental abode, our eternal home.

Yet, despite all our advantages and all the mercy that has been given to us, we are ever prone to become lax and indifferent in devotional service. Although we are offered the greatest opportunity, we neglect our duties and only half-heartedly fulfjll our vows. Our original enthusiasm for Krishna's service is hard to maintain, and if we do so, we think it very laudable, although it is actually only our duty and obligation. We must remember that to whom much is given, much is required. We have certainly been given much transcendental mercy. Let us not be found wanting in our response.

☆☆☆☆☆☆☆☆☆☆☆☆☆☆☆

Meditation 19

Krishna Conscious Living

"A PERSON ACTING in the service of Krishna with his body, mind, and words is a liberated person, even within the material world." (*Bhakti-rasamrita-sindhu*)

Serving Krishna with body, mind, and words is the sure path to liberation. Indeed, one who practices such service is already liberated, although he still appears to have a material body and participate in the normal course of daily affairs. There is a great difference between the activities of a devotee and those of a *karmi*, or worldly man. Because a devotee's life is full of Krishna consciousness, the highest virtue, it is automatically filled with lesser virtues like truthfulness, honesty, tolerance, and compassion. Moreover, because the devotee is free from false ego and identification with the material body, he does not care what others may think; rather, he cares what his spiritual master and Krishna think. After all, man looks externally, but God sees the heart. If we use our body, mind, and words exclusively for His satisfaction and service, our heart will remain pure.

Each day we have to reaffirm our vows and re-dedicate ourselves with the enthusiasm we had upon first encountering Krishna. Daily we ought to pray, "O my Lord, when will my eyes be decorated with tears of love flowing constantly when I chant Your Holy Name? When will my voice choke up, and when will the hairs of my body stand on end at the recitation of Your Holy Name?" (*Sikshastaka* 6) Such tears attract Krishna and guarantee the success of human life.

According to the intensity of our desire, we make progress in Krishna consciousness, but if we desire perfection, we must continue to the end. To be steady in Krishna consciousness is not an easy thing. Even so-called big devotees may fall down due to some hidden defect. What, then, can be said of those who are weak of faith or half-hearted in determination? The deceits of *maya* are doubtlessly many, and even a little inattention in devotional life can wreak havoc with our spiritual progress. Therefore, we must take shelter of regular hearing and chanting to remain always strong in our resolve. It is very dangerous to neglect our vows to the Lord. If we neglect our chanting of rounds, fail to read the holy books, or omit some other devotional practice, we are sure to suffer. If the neglect arises from having to perform some other service, our discipline can again be taken up, but if we abandon our duties out of laziness or desire for sense gratification, our creeper of attachment for the Lord will wither.

Spiritual life is like a razor's edge: used carefully and with expert guidance, it is wonderful, but as soon as we become careless, there is bleeding and injury. We need always be on guard and examine ourselves morning and night. A good practice is to pray to the spiritual master early in the morning and make a vow to perform some service, control a particular passion, or overcome a bad habit such as talking nonsense. Then in the evening, before taking rest, we should again pray to him, and assess our performance, acknowledging his help in success or requesting his forgiveness in defeat.

Let us put on the whole armor of God against the attacks of *maya* by keeping the senses always engaged in devotional service. If we can control our senses, we can more easily control the restless mind. Let us be always absorbed in thoughts of Krishna by reading, writing, chanting, or working for His pleasure. And we should always look for opportunities to inform others about Krishna's glories and Holy Name.

We should, however, avoid the fault of making a show of devotion to receive the praise of men. Sometimes neophyte devotees want to retire from active service to sit down in a holy place and chant meditative *bhajanas* for personal elevation. This is condemned by the pure devotees. For this age, Lord Chaitanya has specifically recommended *sankirtana*, the congregational chanting of the Holy Name, and the vigorous preaching of the glories of the Lord to the innocent public. If we please Him by our sincere endeavor to execute His mission, our own personal destiny will certainly be secured.

If a servant pleases a perfect master, the master automatically takes care of all the needs of the servant. Indeed, the master knows his servant's needs better than the servant himself. Therefore we need not pray for our own salvation, nor for bodily necessities such as food and clothes. Our Master, Lord Krishna, certainly knows what we need and what is good for us. A devotee needs only one prayer: "My dear Lord, how can I serve You?" Such a prayer will never go unanswered.

✧✧✧✧✧✧✧✧✧✧✧✧✧✧✧

Meditation 20

Retiring From The World

"A VAISHNAVA SHOULD always avoid the association of ordinary people. Common people are very much materially attached, especially to sex life. Vaishnavas should also avoid the company of those who are not devotees of Lord Krishna."(*Chaitanya Charitamrita*, Madh. 22:87)

Retiring from the material world entails more than moving to a forest. *Srimad-Bhagavatam* says: "What is the use of going to the forest if you take your six wives with you?" If we do not undergo a change of heart and a change of life, then moving to a new location will not help us, for we will still be controlled by the six senses, including the mind. These senses are compared to uncontrolled wives.

For the neophyte devotee, it is most important to associate with those who are serious for spiritual advancement and avoid those who are not. In the midst of materialists and sexmongers, we can never be inspired to renounce anything, but in the association of sages, we will. We must withdraw ourselves from all unholy association and avoid talking unnecessarily, repeating rumors, wasting time on unimportant things, and reading literatures that do not encourage a devotional life. Thus, we will automatically have plenty of time to think always of the Lord. The human life is a junction in the evolutionary cycle. those who aspire to be godly forsake the worldly; those who cling to the worldly become beastly.

Since time immemorial, saints and sages have advised us to separate ourselves from the world and live a holy life pleasing to God. But where should we go? To the forest or the mountains? How do we find Him who is not seen with mortal eyes but who resides in the hearts of all? For the people in this age, the scriptures do not recommend going to the forest or trying to chant in a secluded place. Rather, they advise giving up the association of non-devotees and living in a place where the Names and pastimes of the Lord are constantly heard. In such an atmosphere we can avoid the degrading conversations that destroy our divine awareness. We can remain secluded even while performing all kinds of Krishna conscious duties, for our home is no longer a house but the temple of God. In the temple of the Lord, we can relish obscurity even while in the public eye, remembering that only the Lord is all-famous. We can be silent and sober, even while singing and dancing before the beautiful form of the Deity. Because we have learned to obey, we can be humble and gentle, even while commanding all to serve Him.

The devotee's real protection is pure love for Krishna, which surpasses the protection of those who live in fear of God. Of course, fear of God is the beginning of wisdom, far better than the vain illusions of the wicked, who are cast again and again into demoniac wombs because of their envy and false pride.

Transcendental love does not allow us to forget Him even for a minute, however, nor to think very highly of ourselves. Our confidence is in Him, not in our own puny abilities. Out of His causeless mercy, Krishna sends us trials and tribulations to protect us from overconfidence, from the tendency to become puffed up, and from the allurement of material comforts.

If only we could overcome the desire for sense gratification and learn not to expect happiness from temporary objects! How peaceful we would be! What a clean conscience we would have! Transcendental bliss is ours if we can just cut ourselves off, once and for all, from empty concerns and absorb ourselves exclusively in thinking of Him and everything related to Him: His Name, paraphernalia, associates, pastimes, and supreme abode.

That transcendental abode is won only by those who have emptied themselves of false ego and false pride. Why do we run here and there looking for bestial pleasures? Why do we wish to see or experience the forbidden? Why not be content with the beauty and wonder that Krishna has kindly given? Do we think that once we attain some special object of desire, we will be satisfied? Impossible! Even if we gain the whole world, we cannot be satisfied, because the world is but an empty dream for the soul.

Therefore, let us lift up our eyes and gaze into Vaikuntha's sky, where the Supreme Personality of Godhead lives eternally with His friends and associates. Let us fix our minds and hearts on that transcendental region from which we never return to this world of birth and death. Let us withdraw ourselves from all the concerns of material life and fix our attention eternally on Him who is the all-attractive Supreme Spirit. He has made Himself easily accessible in the sound of His Holy Name.

Meditation 21

Feelings Of Separation

"O GOVINDA! FEELING Your separation, I am considering a moment to be like twelve years or more. Tears are flowing from my eyes like torrents of rain, and I am feeling all vacant in the world in Your absence." (*Sikshastaka* 7)

People frequently talk about wanting to feel the presence of God, but they are baffled as to how it is possible. Lord Chaitanya, who is Krishna Himself in the guise of a pure devotee, has come to show us how we can always relish the presence of the Lord by feeling His separation. Great devotees such as the Goswamis of Vrindaban were constantly in this mood, always searching for Him, even asking the trees and creepers if they had seen Krishna, the Son of Nanda Maharaj, pass their way. They never presented themselves as confidants of the Lord, nor said, "Oh, we have found God."

Similarly, if we wish to make progress in ecstatic love, we have to increase our hankering for Krishna by strictly following the regulative principles of devotional service. Giving up the desire for freedom, we must control the unbridled senses. We must be grave instead of frivolous. We must cry for Krishna, because yearning for Him brings great relief, whereas levity brings only sorrow.

Yudhisthira Maharaj once said that the greatest wonder is that, although we see everyone around us dying, we still think that we will live forever. There is another wonder: although we are in a place of great danger and misery—a place where birth and death are repeated constantly with the chance of falling into a species of life from which it is impossible to make advancement—we think that we can be happy here. Like animals in a slaughterhouse, we are foolish and ignorant of the danger of our situation. Not appreciating the great opportunity for self-realization that the Lord has given us in this human life, we glide merrily down the primrose path to hell. If only we would remember that no pleasure is genuine if it is not eternal! Though it may seem like nectar in the beginning, the end will surely be bitter poison. What a man sows, he reaps. One is truly happy if he is done with suffering the reactions of sinful life, but happier still if he relishes the joys of devotion to God.

If we are not favored by men, we should not be discouraged. It is undoubtedly the mercy of God, lest we become proud. But we should consider it most regrettable if we are not satisfying the Supreme Lord. For His pleasure, we should be ready to sacrifice everything—even our very life, if necessary. We should live simply and acquire few possessions so that we may possess more love for God. We should be busy in His service, but not in the business of others. We should be patient with others and hard on ourselves. We should fight evil like a valiant son of God and take shelter in spiritual discipline, for habit is broken by habit.

Since the Lord knows our needs, even without our asking, we should accept whatever comes or doesn't come as His mercy. It may be safer and better for us to enjoy less in this world in order to enjoy more in the next. If we learn to relish the pleasure of His Holy Name, we can have unlimited bliss now and forevermore.

Unfortunately, we do not give as much thought to the hereafter as to the here and now. But who would not be more devout if he thought of an early death, rather than a long life? Indeed, even the mundane philosophers of long ago advised us to live each day as if it were our last. Would we care about society, friendship and love if we were to meet our Maker today and have to give an account of our every deed? Could we really go on relishing the gratification of this rotting body if we were aware that tonight we might be confined to the torments of hell? Would not the opportunity to render devotional service appear wonderful then? Our austerities—cold showers, hard work, long hours, and little sleep—would suddenly appear like paradise. But since such reflections do not enter our minds and hearts, we remain attached to sense pleasure and consequently remain indifferent and lax in religious zeal. The body complains so loudly because our soul has been starved into lifelessness.

There is only one thing left. Before it is too late, we must take advantage of the unlimited mercy of Lord Chaitanya, who has given us the loud chanting of the Holy Names of the Lord: Hare Krishna, Hare Krishna, Krishna Krishna, Hare Hare; Hare Rama, Hare Rama, Rama Rama, Hare Hare. Wake up! Wake up! We're sleeping on the lap of the *maya* witch. Wake up! Chant Hare Krishna and be happy.

☆☆☆☆☆☆☆☆☆☆☆☆☆☆☆☆☆

Meditation 22

The Absolute Misery Of Material Existence

"FROM THE HIGHEST planet in the material world down to the lowest, all are places of misery wherein repeated birth and death take place. But one who attains to My abode, O son of Kunti, never takes birth again." (*Bhagavad-gita* 8:16)

Sometimes we think that everyone else enjoys an easy life and great happiness and that we alone are miserable. We should not be deceived. In this world, no one is always happy, but everyone is miserable at times. How can it be otherwise? Death is coming, perhaps this very moment. Exactly when, we don't know, and this adds to our fear. Of course, like an ostrich, we may try to ignore death, but it comes just the same. And then what? "To die; to sleep;—To sleep? Perchance to dream! Ay, there's the rub," Shakespeare writes. "For in that sleep of death what dreams may come, when we have shuffled off this mortal coil, must give us pause." We live in fear, not knowing what lies ahead. Like a child in the dark, we are tormented by the mind and by our ignorance of what the future holds.

Psychologists, psychiatrists, sociologists, and welfare workers try to alleviate these fears. If they could succeed, no one would be afraid, but this is not the case. The world lives in fear, and for good reason.

This material world is a dangerous place, and miserable besides. Birth, death, old age, and disease are our lot in this world. King and pauper, priest and sinner—everyone is bound up by the laws of material nature and remains so until liberated by God or His representative.

Then who is better off—the rich or the poor, the wise or the ignorant, the slave or the free? Without Krishna consciousness, there is no difference. When the ship sinks, all go down. Neither our pedigree nor our friends and relatives nor even our riches will help us. Everyone must swim for himself, and if he doesn't know how, he is lost. Material education devoid of awareness of God is useless baggage, and material possessions are just added weights pulling us down to our doom. What is the profit of possessing the whole world, if we have not learned to protect ourselves from the cruel hand of death? Happiness is impossible here.

On the other hand, one who has learned to be content with whatever the Lord gives is always happy, for he sees his Friend, Lord Krishna, in everything. He knows that the Lord has a superior nature, "which is eternal and is transcendental to this manifested and unmanifested matter. It is supreme and is never annihilated." (*Bg.* 8.20) How foolish are those who are attached to this miserable temporary creation! By the Lord's grace, we can enjoy the unlimitedly blissful Spiritual Sky. It is indeed strange that people willingly accept the kicks of *maya*—working hard day and night, barely securing the necessities of life—and think that they are enjoying. Indeed, they come back again and again, life after life, for more.

Srimad-Bhagavatam calls this "chewing the chewed." Children sometimes chew gum for some time and then spit it out when it is tasteless. What is to be gained by chewing it again? Similarly, the living being, transmigrating through 8,400,000 species of life, enjoys sense gratification in all of them. Why waste the human form of life on the same old thing—eating, sleeping, defending, and mating? Such pleasures are available even to dogs and hogs. Human life is meant for self-realization.

The saints and sages did not look to the pleasures of the body, nor to other sources of mundane enjoyment. Their whole concern was for the eternal. They fixed their gaze on the Kingdom of God and did not look to the right or left. We can follow in their footsteps, if we so desire. As pilgrims, we should not lose heart, nor give up the fight. So long as we have breath, there is yet time. Maharaj Katvanga became fully Krishna conscious in one instant simply by fixing his mind on the Lotus Feet of the Lord. True, we are weak and frail, but this should make us remain humble and avoid the fall of pride. If we become like little children, helpless and trusting, depending fully on God's mercy, He will surely help us. Indeed, if we put our hand in His by loudly chanting His Holy Name, He will lead us on and on, back home, back to Godhead. Hare Krishna!

☆☆☆☆☆☆☆☆☆☆☆☆☆☆

Meditation 23

Death Means Change Of Body

"As the embodied soul continually passes, in this body, from boyhood to youth to old age, the soul similarly passes into another body at death. The self-realized soul is not bewildered by such a change." (*Bhagavad-gita* 2:13)

Death comes for everyone. Its certainty is proverbial: "As sure as death." Lord Krishna further assures us, "I am all-devouring death." (*Bg.* 10:34) It is therefore a great wonder that people in general are unaware that death is coming. Although people are dying every moment, those who are living are thinking, "My friend has died, but I shall live forever." We do not consider that when the sun rises in the morning and sets in the evening, it is actually decreasing the remainder of our life. We are so foolish that when we calculate our age, we say that we are twenty years old, or thirty years old, but it would be more accurate to say that we are twenty or thirty years dead. As soon as we are born, we are allotted so many days, hours, and minutes to live. When this time runs out, we die. No one, not even the greatest doctor or scientist, can prolong his life one second beyond his allotted time.

Very soon we will die. No one can remain here forever. Isn't it strange that we do not prepare for the inevitable future? How foolish and hard of heart we are to think only of mortal life when we can enter into an eternal life of bliss and knowledge!

Therefore, we are advised to live every moment, every thought and deed, as if it were our last. By doing so, we would complete many tasks still undone, and leave undone many things we ought never have considered. In this way, we would have a good conscience and not fear death. After all, if we are not prepared to die today, what makes us think that we will be ready tomorrow? Besides, when death comes, it will not be tomorrow, but today. Now is the acceptable time. Now is the day for enlightened action and liberation.

Even if we live three score and ten years, or even ten score and three, that is no guarantee of happiness. There are trees that live for thousands of years. A long duration of life has no intrinsic value. Life is meant for serving God. Even a moment spent in the association of a pure devotee, or in rendering unmotivated service to the Lord, is enough to send us all the way back home, back to Godhead. It is not the quantity of life that counts, but the quality. Should we think that a drunkard who happens to live for ninety years has a more valuable life than that of Lord Chaitanya who lived for only forty-eight, or that of Lord Jesus, who died on the cross at thirty-three? If we could live but one day as They lived, a glorious destiny would be assured.

Unfortunately, our nature is forgetfulness. Although we all know that many people die suddenly and quite unexpectedly, we carry on in our usual humdrum way, as if all were well. When our final moment comes, however, we may think differently of that life which will then be over. There is often much regret and remorse that the boon of human life has been carelessly wasted.

The present is most precious. Now is the time of action, of sowing, and the harvest of reactions is entirely up to us. If we sow to the flesh, we will reap rotting flesh, but if we realize that we are not the material body, and therefore sow to the spirit soul, we will reap a spiritual body like unto the Lord's. Remembering that the moment of death is always at hand, we should be motivated tó become detached from sense pleasure. Remembering that the moment of death for this body can actually be the moment of liberation and entrance into the Spiritual Sky in a body of eternity, knowledge, and bliss, we should feel happy rather than sad. Therefore, we should learn to deny the material body now, spurn all material things, and purify ourselves by austerity and penance to enjoy a transcendental life eternally.

Oh, what fools we are! We plan for happiness here, but in a second everything is finished. Who will remember us then? Who will help us? When death comes, it is too late to change. Either for good or ill, the die is cast, and we are forced by eternal time to accept our destiny, our *karma*. Let us therefore act to assure the soul's safe passage to the Kingdom of God. Let us accumulate possessions that are not of this world so that we will not have to go empty handed. Let us think of nothing but God's eternal abode, and the only means to get there—pure love of God. Let us make friends with His devotees so that we, in turn, may become like them by following in their footsteps.

☆☆☆☆☆☆☆☆☆☆☆☆☆☆☆☆☆

Meditation 24

Reward And Punishment

"IN PROPORTION TO the extent of one's religious or irreligious actions in this life, one must enjoy or suffer the corresponding reactions of his *karma* in the next." (*Srimad-Bhagavatam* 6:1:45)

Lord Krishna explains in *Bhagavad-gita* that those who act in the mode of goodness ascend to the heavenly planetary systems to enjoy godly delights, those who behave in ordinary ways and avoid excessive sinful activity remain in the middle or earthly regions, and those who perform abominable and prohibited actions are degraded to hellish life. We should not ignorantly think that we can fool God or that we will not be caught and punished for our offenses. The scriptures explain that there are many witnesses to our activities: the sun is witness by day and the moon by night, the demigods and higher beings are witnesses because they are the controllers of our senses, and ultimately, the Supreme Personality of Godhead is witness as the Supersoul in our heart. Therefore, we should always consider the consequences of our actions. There is one way that seems pleasant for a season, but the end is death. Its beginning is as sweet as honey, but its end is as bitter as poison. There is another way that is difficult and unpleasant to start, but its end is ambrosial nectar and life eternal. We are always on one of these paths.

The choice is ours which road to take. If we choose wisely, there is life, and if we choose wrongly, there is death. And after death, the judgement. In death's court, the evidence is complete, rendering absolute justice, with no chance of bribery or excuse. Nothing will remain hidden, and we will be known as we are. No privacy, no secrecy. Death knows all. But that will terrify us only if our motives are impure and our actions reprehensible. For those who are pure in heart and clean in deed, it is the greatest relief to know that they will never be misjudged again, as the saintly frequently are in this world. Besides that, if we don't atone now for our sins and abandon every evil way, we will have to pay point for point in the future.

How we deceive ourselves by love of this flesh! We do not realize that these senses are the source of all misery. Whatever pain or suffering we have ever endured exists only because we identify with this combination of blood, pus, urine, and stool, which we lovingly call "my body." O enemy of the soul, if only we could sever that connection as easily as one severs the umbilical cord at birth! Alas, because it is desire that binds us, only desire can liberate us. Unfortunately, because our desire for liberation is usually not very strong, we are forced to accept birth again and again in this material world.

God's justice is always perfect. Every evil deed is recompensed with its proper punishment. Those who steal another's wife, children, or money are put into the hell called Tamisra, where they are continually beaten, starved, and denied water. Still, they cannot die. Those who are under the spell of illusion, identifying themselves with the body and bodily extensions like the family—working hard to satisfy them, but also inflicting pain and violence on others—are forced to enter the Raurava hell. There, the injured appear as animals and inflict very severe pain upon the transgressors. The hell called Kumbhipaka awaits those who maintain their bodies and satisfy their tongues by cooking poor animals and birds alive. In this hell they in turn are cooked in boiling oil. Cruel-hearted rulers and government men who harass and injure innocent people are tormented in the hell known as

Kukharamukha by being crushed between stones, just as sugar cane is squeezed in a press. There are also hells for thieves, where their skin is torn from their body and they are cut into tiny pieces again and again. Fornicators are punished in another hell by being beaten with whips and forced to embrace male or female forms of red-hot iron. Those who like to drink liquor are forced to drink burning liquid iron.

Unbelievers may laugh, but no one will laugh on judgement day. God is not mocked. What a man sows, he reaps. Is it not better that we learn to endure small things now, rather than suffer greatly in the future? If we cannot tolerate a little inconvenience now, even for the sake of self-realization to gain the eternal Kingdom of God, how will we be able to endure the torments of hell? If a little austerity and penance seem too difficult now, what of the reaction we will have to suffer hereafter for our many offenses? Now is the time to choose. We cannot serve two masters, or set our faces in two directions.

One who develops his love for Krishna does not fear death, hell, justice, or anything else. The cat carries the kitten and the rat in the same mouth, but for the kitten, the cat's mouth is comforting, whereas for the rat, it is death personified. If we love God, we have no fear, but if we love sin, we cannot avoid fear.

Fear of God and His punishment is not necessary for His surrendered souls. Fear exists to keep miscreants from breaking His laws and going to hell, and that is also good. If we chant His Holy Name with faith and attention, however, we can avoid sinful activity and develop pure love for Him, which is far better than fearing Him. Let us therefore chant Hare Krishna and be fearless.

☆☆☆☆☆☆☆☆☆☆☆☆☆☆☆☆☆

Meditation 25

Pressing On The Upward Path

"THE VERDICT OF all revealed scriptures is that by even a moment's association with a pure devotee, one can attain all success." (*Chaitanya Charitamrita*, Madh. 22:54)

Spiritual reformation requires determination and seriousness. There is no time to lose, and it is too dangerous to gamble in the usual trial-and-error experimental fashion. Therefore, the *Mundaka Upanisad* advises us to learn the transcendental science by approaching a bona fide spiritual master in discipular succession, a master who is fixed in the Absolute Truth. We should avoid foolish mental speculators, for they will simply waste our time. Even a moment spent with a pure devotee is enough to revolutionize our consciousness and redirect our life. Our beloved spiritual master, His Divine Grace A. C. Bhaktivedanta Swami Prabhupada, had such an experience at His first meeting with His Guru Maharaj in 1922. In just one instant, Srila Prabhupada was convinced of the importance of Lord Chaitanya's desire to spread Krishna consciousness worldwide. He later accomplished this mission.

Such determination is possible when we diligently take to the authorized process of devotional service, always keeping in mind our dissatisfaction with the material world. We should never approach the holy teacher for material benedictions, for he is able to give us something infinitely more valuable—spiritual perfection. By rendering service to him and making relevant inquiry, we can soon reap the greatest of rewards: freedom from fear and sorrow, positive attachment to Krishna, and transcendental happiness on the devotional path. With only a little endeavor, we soon find great peace and joy, as well as real knowledge. God is the abundant rewarder of those who diligently seek Him. It is good to be reasonably confident of attaining Krishna's abode, but let us not act as though it were our right, lest we grow lazy and proud.

Spiritual life is a matter of cultivation, and cultivation means hard work. Of course, for an advanced devotee, there is no work at all. Everything is a labor of love. But in the neophyte stage, devotional service may sometimes seem like difficult work. Sometimes, we may find ourselves thinking, "Is it worth it? Will I really ever make it?" Dear soul, if you knew the answer to that question, what would you do then? Just do that now, and all will be well. We should stand on the promise of the highest authority, Lord Krishna Himself, that we can succeed if we but surrender to Him. Lord Krishna told Arjuna to declare it boldly: "My devotee will never perish." There is no need to waste time speculating about the future. It is far better to be enthusiastic in the execution of our duty for His satisfaction, and leave the future to Him.

Two points are very important for rapid advancement in Krishna consciousness. One is negative, the other positive. We must—forcibly if necessary—avoid the four pillars of sinful activity: illicit sex, intoxication, animal slaughter, and gambling. Of these, illicit sex—or even its desire—leads to the greatest bondage, producing a lust that burns like fire and pushes us to bestial acts of sensuality. Animalistic living makes us forget our divine nature and spiritual duty. Positively, we must always remember the Personality of Godhead by chanting His Holy Name, hearing about His transcendental pastimes, eating remnants of foodstuffs offered to Him in love and devotion, and associating with His pure devotees. The more fervently we follow these simple regulations, the more quickly we will obtain complete success and the mercy of the Lord.

Everything is based on desire. Due to desire for sense gratification we have fallen into this ocean of material life; when we have only transcendental desire, we will dive deeply into the ocean of nectar called devotional service. A humble devotee naturally accepts the orders of his spiritual master as his life and soul and executes them to the best of his ability. A half-hearted devotee remains lukewarm in his commitment and thus experiences difficulty after difficulty. He suffers misery on every side, for he is unable to taste the bliss of Krishna consciousness and he is afraid to enjoy the lusts of the flesh. An unfaithful devotee suffers as if he were the most wretched of men. Although he knows better, he lacks the character to improve. He is always unhappy.

How much more sublime to accept a life of plain living and high thinking! We should neglect the society of the world; eat only necessary and healthy *prasadam*, spiritual food cooked with love and devotion for the Lord; take no care to dress the body luxuriously, but mark it and treat it as the temple of God; work hard for His satisfaction; speak only what is necessary and elevating; read the holy books; chant the Holy Name; and always think of Krishna. If we never did anything but this, how much happier and content we would be! Unfortunately, being slaves to the senses, we are dragged into every abominable condition and, eventually, into hell.

When we finally recognize no shelter other than Krishna, we will begin to find Him, and when nothing else satisfies, we will relish His association perfectly. Then material things will no longer disturb us, and we will neither lament for something lost nor hanker for some gain, neither rejoice for the pleasant nor grieve over the unpleasant. In all things we will surrender to His will and place ourselves completely and confidently in His hands. He never fails to give His devotee protection.

☆☆☆☆☆☆☆☆☆☆☆☆☆☆☆☆☆

Meditation 26

Finding Our True Love Within

"Pure love for Krishna is eternally established in the hearts of living entities. It is not something to be gained from another source. When the heart is purified by hearing and chanting, the living entity naturally awakens." (*Chaitanya Charitamrita*, Madh. 22:107)

People often say, "The Kingdom of God is within you," but few have found it. Why? In truth, we do not know how to look for it. The Kingdom of God is not found by material search, nor taken by force of arms, dry speculation, or academic research. The Lord is affectionately known as Bhaktavatsala, the Friend of His devotee. As such, He is conquered only by love and devotion. We must turn to God with our whole heart, forsaking this material world and all its illusions of pleasure, and take refuge in Him alone. He fulfills all our desires.

The Lord is very kind in agreeing to reside in our hearts, but if we want to establish communion with Him, we have to show our love by making our hearts a fit place for His habitation. He delights in a pure heart and a humble spirit, and is moved to compassion when we become absolutely dependent on Him. Although He is far removed from those who take pride in material advancement, He is most intimate with a soul poor in the things of this world but rich in love of God.

We must give way, then, to His divine grace and open wide the portals of spiritual association, shutting out all else. What more do we need? Because He is full in all opulences—wealth, fame, beauty, knowledge, strength, and renunciation—He is called Krishna, the all-attractive. Knowing perfectly what we need or want, He will provide it according to His own infinite wisdom. With such a great Friend, why should we court the favor of others? Since neither men nor demigods are independent or able to deliver us from the cycle of birth and death, we should not put much confidence or hope in them. They can neither grant us the ultimate good, nor impede us beyond what God Almighty allows. We need not fear those who can kill the body, but we should fear being put into a condition in which we cannot remember Lord Krishna. Everything is under His control. Those who oppose us today may help us tomorrow, and vice versa. If we act for His satisfaction, we will always remain above the dualities of this world and gradually ascend the transcendental path back home, back to Godhead.

Thus we should always be mindful that we have no permanent home here. The spirit soul is a foreigner to this mortal land and can never rest this side of our Vaikuntha home. Why are we so allured by the glitter of this world? For one life of devotional service, we can gain unending ecstasy in Krishna's eternal abode. The illusions of this world must pass away, and our present existence with it. Unless we detach ourselves from all things temporal, we will again be entangled in death and rebirth. Therefore, let us fix our minds on Krishna without deviation. He has promised that if we do so, we will surely come to Him.

Fixing the mind on the Supreme may be difficult for those who do not know that the Lord has form, but it is most easy and natural for His devotee. The Lord descends from time to time just to display His eternal pastimes of bliss, and even a neophyte can obtain the perfect result by thinking of them. Then what of those who are always immersed in the chanting of His Holy Name and fame with ardent devotion? Their success is guaranteed, for there is no difference between God and His name, fame, pastimes, and entourage. Since He is absolute, everything connected to Him is absolute. If somehow or other we are fortunate enough to come in contact with Him, we become fixed in His eternal loving play. Then we will not care a fig for the dreamlike pleasures of mundane society and love. Nor will we care for the sufferings or reproaches endured for the sake of our beloved. Love of God is so satisfying that once we have tasted it, we will never be able to live without it.

☆☆☆☆☆☆☆☆☆☆☆☆☆☆☆☆

Meditation 27

Genuine Humility

"I AM NOT a *brahmana*, I am not a *kshatriya*, I am not a *vaishya* or a *sudra*. Nor am I a *brahmachari*, a householder, a *vanaprastha* or a *sannyasi*. I identify Myself only as the servant of the servant of the servant of the Lotus Feet of Lord Sri Krishna, the maintainer of the *gopis*." (*Chaitanya Charitamrita*, Madh. 13:80)

Generally people identify themselves with their family, society, business, and material possessions and are especially attached to wealth, aristocracy, education, and personal beauty. All these different opulences, however, have nothing to do with the spirit soul.

Why does Lord Chaitanya describe Himself as servant of the servant of the servant? Who wants to be a servant, what to speak of being a servant of a servant? Lord Chaitanya, exhibiting Himself as the greatest devotee, is emphasizing that those who want to advance in Krishna consciousness must become as humble as grass. If we are to attract the recognition of Lord Krishna, we must give up the false pride of the body and find real pleasure in being the eternal servant of the Lord. Indeed, the Lord is even more pleased when we become the servant of His servant. The spiritual master, being the most confidential servant of the Lord, deserves our best service, and we should strive to become his most obedient and menial assistant in the Lord's mission. That is the sure path to success. No one can approach God directly, but He is easily attained through His pure devotee.

In this regard, we should not be agitated by external circumstances, nor by personal attacks, but take care always to please God and His representative. There are many practical guidelines in this matter. Keeping a clean conscience is the best way to feel God's protection. The malice of common men cannot harm us if we have received the shelter of Krishna, nor can all of the efforts of great men help us if God wills otherwise. If we can learn to be tolerant now, without complaining, we will soon know His divine grace. God knows us through and through and knows what we can bear, just as an expert smith knows how much fire is required to refine gold. We must trust Him. He never makes a mistake. We must have faith in His promise to bring us to perfection.

But if we are serious about accepting His help, we must also be willing to take the help of His servants. Thus, we are advised to admit our shortcomings and reveal our doubts to those who are in a position to help. This will increase our humility and make us determined to avoid temptations in the future. Besides this, admission of weakness is the greatest antidote for the disappointment and anger of others.

We should remember that it is the humble devotee who obtains the Lord's causeless mercy and finds the door to devotional service wide open. It is he who is liberated even within this lifetime. Only one who has learned to humble himself becomes a candidate for God's love and consolation. When one is humiliated before men for the Lord's sake, the Lord raises him up to great glory. God is inclined towards the humble in spirit, and He gives Himself without reservation to those who prostrate themselves before Him. Thus, the humble soul finds peace in Lord Krishna's loving service, and neither material obstacles nor spiritual aspirations can draw his attention away from the nectar of Krishna's Lotus Feet.

✰✰✰✰✰✰✰✰✰✰✰✰✰✰✰✰✰

Meditation 28

Freedom From Fear

"DEVOTEES SOLELY ENGAGED in the devotional service of the Supreme Personality of Godhead, Narayana, never fear any condition of life. For them the heavenly planets, liberation and the hellish planets are all the same, for such devotees are interested only in the service of the Lord." (*Srimad-Bhagavatam* 6:17:28)

A great politician once said, "The only thing we have to fear is fear itself." These words may have won him public acclaim, but not freedom from the dread of old age, disease, and death. Material existence is a very fearful condition: there is danger at every step. Death lurks for all who live in mortal frames and will not allow even a king prolonged peace of mind. Only a devotee—knowing himself as different from the material body, as part and parcel of the Lord—can be completely fearless. A devotee knows both himself and the Supreme Self to be eternal, subject neither to birth nor death nor any other material condition. Thus the devotee and his Lord live together in perfect harmony. Truly, it is better to be an illiterate devotee than a learned fool, and better to act faithfully in the sight of God than to be esteemed by multitudes of fools.

Faith means unlimited trust in God, whatever the circumstances. By faith, we can avoid many sources of disturbance. God does everything perfectly; we, by our misuse of independence, make it imperfect. We should suspect our own motives but not those of others. By always striving to work diligently and enthusiastically for Krishna, we can encourage others to do the same. Leaving undone what is unholy, we should accomplish every God-given duty. Talking little, we should speak only what is beneficial and necessary. A gross materialist is suspicious of everyone because he himself is not trustworthy. His goal is leisure, not service. Speaking only nonsense, he does not accomplish anything or make progress toward life's ultimate goal.

Therefore, with the help of God, as given in the scripture and in the person of the bona fide spiritual master, we should focus upon ourselves. "Physician heal thyself." If we do not develop good qualities, how can we expect others to? The word *acharya* refers to one who teaches by example. A teacher who does not practice what he preaches may succeed in the material world, where practically everyone is cheating or being cheated, but he will never be respected in the society of devotees. We cannot cover our own deficiencies with excuses unacceptable from others. If we wish to teach forbearance, we must joyfully tolerate injustice to ourselves. A man of real knowledge and detachment is free from the urge to criticize others and is always critical of himself.

We cannot claim any great credit if we live amiably with the gentle and good. After all, their association is desired by almost everyone. But one who remains peaceful and cheerful in the midst of crude and demoniac persons who are by nature undisciplined and irritating, is virtue personified.

By right endeavor, we should obtain that peace which surpasses all material understanding. Then we will be peaceful anywhere and everywhere, be it heaven or hell, and in all conditions, liberated or otherwise. Devotional service to the Lord is so transcendentally soothing that a devotee loses all material consciousness. He does not hanker for anything in this world. Just as the Ganges flows toward the sea with irresistible force, so the mind of a devotee is drawn to Krishna without being diverted to anything else. Such results are certain if we but seek the association of pure devotees and go on hearing and chanting about the wonderful pastimes and activities of the Supreme Lord. Discussions about Krishna are pleasing and satisfying to the ear and the heart. They bring us perfect peace.

☆☆☆☆☆☆☆☆☆☆☆☆☆☆☆

Meditation 29

A Pure Mind With Singleness Of Purpose

"PEACEFULNESS, SELF-CONTROL, AUSTERITY, purity, tolerance, honesty, wisdom, knowledge and religiousness—these are the qualities by which the *brahmanas* work." (*Bhagavad-gita* 18:42)

The qualities of a *brahmana* are in the mode of goodness. Unlike the modes of passion and ignorance, goodness elevates us gradually to the position of seeing things as they are, in pure Krishna consciousness. Therefore, the Lord advises us to be always situated in goodness.

Goodness has two underlying characteristics: simplicity and purity.

If our motives are pure and our endeavors sincere and uncomplicated by duplicity, we will surely find ourselves coming closer to God, who is the Supreme Pure and the ultimate unity in diversity.

When our aims are duplicitous and our methods sophisticated, our life becomes a complicated affair, but when we are pure in heart and straightforward in our dealings, nothing is perplexing and no good act is difficult to perform. Certainly, if we seek nothing but the Kingdom of God, and strive only for God's satisfaction, our soul will enjoy perfect freedom from all anxiety and material contamination.

How wonderful is the creation of Lord Krishna! It is just like a great holy book, teaching us His ways. He is the beginning, the middle, and the end of all things. If we but have the eyes, we can see Him reflected in each and every particle. Moreover, He is found in everyone's heart. Yes, God can be seen, but only by those who have smeared their eyes with the salve of love. With such love we can behold our beloved at every instant, for we can behold Him in every creature, and in the sound of His Name: Hare Krishna, Hare Krishna, Krishna Krishna, Hare Hare, Hare Rama, Hare Rama, Rama Rama, Hare Hare.

When by the cleansing process of the Holy Name we become truly good and pure, we will see all things as they are, in relationship to Him. Thus we will understand correctly that He is the origin of all. In Him, everything is good, even passion and ignorance, because He is all good, perfect and transcendental.

We judge a thing by our vision. When we look through colored glasses, everything appears tinted. Because we see through imperfect senses, everything appears imperfect, but when we come to the Absolute Truth and look through the eyes of the scriptures and holy teachers, we can see all things in truth. By foregoing our own imperfect, limited perspective in favor of the unlimited perfection of divine sight, we can attain the greatest joy and relief.

Iron is undoubtedly metal, but in contact with fire, it loses its metallic quality and gradually takes on the qualities of fire. First it is hot, then red hot, and finally, glowing white. Then, whenever it is touched, there is fire. Similarly, the living being takes birth in this body of flesh and bones, materially conditioned by birth, old age, disease, and death. But by contact with the Supreme Lord—through the agency of His pure devotee, the bona fide spiritual master—we can gradually transcend our material conditioning, especially the lower modes of passion and ignorance, and assume the nature of pure spirit—eternity, knowledge, and bliss. Simply by hearing and chanting the transcendental name and glories of the Lord under the direction of God's representative, we can have a new life—a second birth, a birth in Krishna consciousness—and thereby behold the Personality of Godhead face to face.

☆☆☆☆☆☆☆☆☆☆☆☆☆☆☆☆☆☆

Meditation 30

Conquering The Mind

"FOR HIM WHO has conquered the mind, the mind is the best of friends; but for one who has failed to do so, his very mind will be the greatest enemy." (*Bhagavad-gita 6:6*)

Even if someone can understand that he is not the gross material body, he will probably think that he is the mind. Thinking that we are the mind, which is actually the subtle material body, we become attached to it and serve its demands. Neither divine grace nor transcendental realization, however, are products of the mind, nor do they come to those who are imprisoned by the mind's control. Whatever natural insight we have for spiritual life will surely be nullified by an unbridled mind. We may not even be aware of our bondage, so insidious is its control, but the effect is evident by our spiritual blindness, by our misbehavior, and by our rationalizations. We mistake passion for zeal and cannot distinguish between the important and unimportant, between what ought to be done, and what ought to be left undone. While criticizing others for small errors, we overlook greater ones in ourselves. We are well aware of our own feelings but are insensitive to those of others. If we could only see ourselves as others see us and always act wisely with determination, we would be too busy to much notice what others are doing.

The man who seriously desires self-realization must tend to himself first and then to others. If we wish to remove the splinter from someone else's eye, we had best remove the patch from our own first. "Judge not that ye be not judged." It is better not to speak if all that we say is nonsense. Of course, it is best to speak words of transcendental wisdom by which we can elevate ourselves and others to the platform of pure Krishna consciousness. Indeed, that is the way to become free from all bad habits. When we are absorbed in love of God, we are too busy rendering devotional service to fall prey to material absurdity.

The mind is so unstable and flickering that it can convince us that heaven is hell and hell heaven. Therefore, we must be guided by transcendental intelligence. As the leader of the senses, the mind should engage the senses in Krishna's service, but if the mind is uncontrolled, the senses will also be uncontrolled and engaged in serving *maya*, or illusion. Where are our thoughts when we are not thinking devoutly of the Lord? Are the eyes not telling us to look here, to see that? Are our ears not demanding to listen to this thing or that? The tongue is also pulling us in various directions for immediate satisfaction, and the genitals are pushing us to that momentary release that is the ultimate cause of material bondage. Therefore Lord Krishna advises us again and again to control the mind by always thinking of Him. By chanting His Holy

Name and meditating on His transcendental form and activities, we can remain fixed in Krishna consciousness.

We can make rapid progress in self-realization by using the two-edged sword of transcendental knowledge and detachment from sense gratification. This sword is the byproduct of love of God. By it, we can quickly learn to distinguish matter from spirit and thus find ourselves in our original pure Krishna consciousness. Being thus freed from all illusion, we will not attach value to the things of this world, nor consider anything to be great, pleasant, or good, save the Lord's transcendental loving service. We will not want any shelter other than Krishna, for everything else is inferior to Him. Being fully satisfied in His association and considering ourselves to have gained what is beyond all measure and price, we will see that there is nothing more to be desired.

✫✫✫✫✫✫✫✫✫✫✫✫✫

Meditation 31

Pleasing God Removes All Doubts

"O BEST AMONG the twiceborn, it is therefore concluded that the highest perfection one can achieve, by discharging his prescribed duties [*dharma*] according to caste divisions and order of life, is to please the Lord Hari." (*Srimad-Bhagavatam* 1: 2:13)

Some of the byproducts of Krishna conscious living are peace of mind, clear thinking and a clean conscience. Without these, no one can be happy. If we are sure that we have done the right thing, we can be confident even in confusing circumstances, and we can be joyful through all kinds of adversity. A God-conscious person is single minded in purpose, whereas a materialistic man is double minded, and therefore unstable in all his ways.

Having surrendered everything to the Lord, a devotee always remains calm, even though very active in Krishna's service. He is free from duality and doubt, sensual desire and fear. Although demons brag of their fearlessness, defying God and His laws, in due course of time they are inevitably cut down. "The mills of God grind slowly, but they grind exceeding fine." Greece, Rome, Carthage—where are they now? Alexander, Napoleon, Stalin—where have they gone? Can anyone say how they fare today? Is it not better to be the most humble servant of the Lord, than the King of Hell?

Those who really want to achieve peace of mind take no thought for the things of this world nor for tomorrow. The same Lord who provides and protects today will also care and provide tomorrow. When we are protected by the Supreme Great, why should we care for the praise or blame of mere mortals? Whatever benediction they can give is only temporary, and always accompanied by its opposite: if today they award some pleasure, in the future there will be pain. Therefore an intelligent man does not hanker for such benedictions. Indeed, he who does so is certainly foolish.

The praise of men can add nothing to our Krishna consciousness, nor can their criticism detract from it. It is to Krishna alone that we must ultimately answer, and He knows our heart. If God is satisfied, everyone else is satisfied. As soon as we take birth, we have many obligations and responsibilities—to our family, society, our forefathers, and the saints and sages from whom we receive so many benedictions—and if we fail to discharge them, we have to pay our debt in another life. But if we please Krishna, we automatically satisfy all His parts and parcels. This is the easiest and best process, and it will give us the most profound peace.

☆☆☆☆☆☆☆☆☆☆☆☆☆☆

Meditation 32

Perfect Love

"THE PURE DEVOTEE is always within the core of My heart, and I am always in the heart of the pure devotee. My devotees do not know anything else but Me, and I do not know anyone else but them." (*Srimad-Bhagavatam* 9:4:68)

Pure love is not to be found in the material world. Being temporal and defective, our present affections jump from one object to another, always hoping for complete satisfaction, but always disappointed. The final disappointment is death, which ends all hope. Fortunate is he, therefore, who understands the value of love of God and despises its perverted reflection. Indeed, true divine love can never be found where there is even a trace of material affection.

This singular quality of true love is further defined in the *Mahabharata*, when Bhishma says that love means to repose all one's affections in one person. Such love entails absolute surrender of the lover to the beloved. But such love cannot exist among those who identify with material bodies and are prisoners of the senses, which always cry for their own gratification. When we turn our love to Krishna, however, and give up all other loves for His, we find the Perfect Lover who is second to none.

Love for anything material is both deceitful and unsteady, whereas the spiritual reality is true and eternal. Attachment to the mundane brings certain rebirth, but clinging to Krishna assures our final liberation. Then let us love Him and be free; let us make Him our Friend and never be lonely. He has promised never to leave us or forsake us. He will preserve what we have and provide what we lack. Even in death, He will be there, not as Death Personified—as He is for the miscreants—but as our dearmost Friend who has come to take us back home, back to Godhead.

He assures us that if we keep Him always in the core of our hearts, we will also be in His. But if our hearts are already occupied by others, He will never reside there. He will be satisfied only when it is His alone, and He has been unconditionally installed as Lord of our life.

Let us not misjudge Him. It is not that He is jealous or envious like ordinary men. This relationship is a transcendental exclusiveness, whose reciprocal ecstasy can be known only by a surrendered soul. When He is the only one in our hearts, He makes each one of us His sole object of affection. Thus it appears to each *gopi* that Krishna is with her alone and to Lord Jesus Christ that He is the only begotten son of God. The Lord wants each of us to be His only beloved, as He is our only beloved, and, in this way, demonstrate the truth that as we surrender to Him, He rewards us accordingly.

The power of illusion always seeks to divert us from that final leap of faith, telling us we will lose too much. But really, what have we to lose? If we surrender what is already His—as everything is—what have we lost? What is the purpose of a pauper offering another's wealth in charity? Empty-handed we come to the world, and empty-handed we leave. Why do we claim, "This is mine, and that is yours"? Everything belongs to Krishna, the Supreme Personality of Godhead. To surrender everything to Him is to be only honest.

It is time for us to forsake this world of illusion, which is all vanity. The promises of men and the consolations of women are all quite worthless. We are sure to be deceived if we continue to look to our imperfect senses for guidance, but if we turn to the Master of the senses, the Supreme Lord, and to His bona fide representative, the spiritual master, we will surely find the light of life. That torchlight of knowledge by which all ignorance is destroyed shines in the heart of the sincere devotee who chants the Holy Name of the Lord with faith and devotion.

☆☆☆☆☆☆☆☆☆☆☆☆☆☆☆☆

Meditation 33

Being The Lord's Intimate Friend

"THAT VERY ANCIENT science of the relationship with the Supreme is today told by Me to you because you are My devotee as well as My friend; therefore you can understand the transcendental mystery of this science." (*Bhagavad-gita* 4:3)

God is equal to all, yet He becomes the Friend of His devotee, and the enemy of those who hate Him. At first this may seem contradictory, but it is not. Being the all good Father and well-wisher of every living entity, God is simply fulfilling the desires of everyone. If we want to be His friend and demonstrate it by surrendering to Him, He becomes a Friend who is closer than any brother. And if we are envious of Him and want to decry His supreme authority, He allows us to pursue our foolishness. In the end, however, our very desire destroys us. What a great mistake! Krishna has given us all facility to know and love Him, but due to our rebellious attitude we do not take advantage of our opportunity. Woe to us! To whom much is given, much is required.

If others had been as fortunate as we, they would have taken to Krishna consciousness long ago and perfected their lives by devotional service. Nature does not waste her energies; what is not used is taken away. An unused limb soon atrophies, an unused brain soon becomes sluggish, and human life not used for developing Krishna consciousness is soon lost. That is the law of nature. Animals are given complete facility for a life of sense enjoyment, but an animal's pleasures are not meant for man.

Now that we have this human form of life, let us be wise and try to understand that God is very near. Of course, He is near to everyone and everything. As the Supersoul, He is within the hearts of all living entities, and even within and between the atoms. But only in the human form can one become conscious of Him; therefore, Krishna is near in a special way for human beings. If we just chant His Holy Name, we can see. We will feel His presence, and then nothing will be difficult or disturbing. Just by thinking of His pastimes, we can understand that He is never absent from His devotee. By hearing from His representative, the bona fide spiritual master, we can hear Him speaking directly to us, within and without.

How wonderful that the Lord personally speaks the transcendental science to His devotee! It does not matter whether one is a Sanskrit scholar or an illiterate peasant, or whether one is rich or poor. Krishna is attracted only by loving devotional service rendered without price and without hope. But what a reward He offers! This transcendental knowledge, a pearl without price, is Krishna Himself, the nectar for which we are always hankering and the antidote for the burning we feel in the wasteland of material consciousness. With Him, life has beauty, harmony, and meaning; without Him, it is a relentless, hard struggle for existence. With His protection, no one can harm us; without it, no one can save us.

To have Krishna as our Friend is the greatest treasure. One who forgets Him loses more than this whole world is worth. Better to be poor in this life and rich eternally than to have treasures now but nothing hereafter. Therefore, let us make Krishna our only desire, that He who fulfills all desires may reward us unlimitedly with everlasting happiness.

Having Krishna as our Friend means knowing how to please Him. It is commonly said that he who would have friends must first be a friend. We must learn how to satisfy the Lord from the Lord's most confidential friend, the spiritual master. We must learn to offer Krishna foods that He likes, cooked with love and devotion. In *Bhagavad-gita* the Lord asks us to offer Him a leaf, a flower, a little fruit, or water. He never asks for meat, fish, or eggs, since Krishna declares Himself to be the Father and Well-wisher of every living entity. We should note that food must be offered with love and devotion, which are manifested through humility and cleanliness. As He is attracted by love, He is hidden by envy. How unfortunate are those who lose His association due to ignorance and envy! Not knowing that He is the Soul of all souls, the Self of ourselves, they foolishly pursue the phantasmagoria of material dreams and miss the reality of His eternal love.

Let us love Him with a special love reserved for Him alone. Love for others is also good when connected with Him and His service; without reference to Him, however, there is no love, but only lust and illusion. Seeing everyone as part and parcel of our Beloved, we love both friends and foes in Him. Our aim, then, is to bring everyone to the perfect knowledge and love of Him who has become our all in all. Here is perfect unity in diversity. It is not that we ignorantly declare everyone to be God, but that in God we see everyone harmoniously engaged in service to the Whole.

☆☆☆☆☆☆☆☆☆☆☆☆☆☆☆☆

Meditation 34

Thoughts On Tolerance

"O SON OF Kunti, the nonpermanent appearance of happiness and distress, and their disappearance in due course, are like the appearance and disappearance of winter and summer seasons. They arise from sense perception, O scion of Bharata, and one must learn to tolerate them without being disturbed." (*Bhagavad-gita* 2:1)

In the course of our spiritual life, we are asked to tolerate many things. Even in material life, we have no recourse but to tolerate inconveniences. A baby, being unable to communicate, has to submit to his mother's occasional negligence or lack of understanding of his needs; a student has to endure the apparently useless demands of his teachers; a worker has to suffer the demands of his boss; a lover bears willingly the eccentricities of the beloved. No one likes it, but we must be tolerant in order to get the results we desire. Similarly, if we are serious about realizing ourselves as spirit souls, different from the material body, we have to train our senses by subjugation. This requires tolerance.

What we endure in order to obtain our sense gratification may not be good for us or any one else. For instance, a woman may tolerate the sexual advances of her employer in order to get a promotion, but this is detrimental to both parties. Nor will either one feel truly satisfied.

Temporary pleasure does not last, and it is replaced by remorse and grief. Tolerance in the execution of Krishna consciousness, however, is always beneficial.

Resisting evil, acting properly even when it is very difficult, is always rewarding, not only in this life but also in the future. Indeed, when one is actually advanced in spiritual understanding, those things that were formerly difficult become easy, and those things that once caused distress, disappointment, and frustration become occasions for experiencing the direct mercy of the Lord. That is the test of a first-class devotee: he sees everything—the good or the bad, the pleasant or the unpleasant, success or failure—as coming from his dear Friend, Lord Krishna. Because the devotee is always in touch with the Lord, he is in a constant state of transcendental bliss. For him, the concept of tolerance has more or less become meaningless. It is the greatest pleasure to tolerate hardships for Krishna.

Still, for the neophyte devotee, tolerance is not always easy. When some reverse or calamity is experienced, he thinks, "This is due to my past offenses, and when I have atoned for my sin, it will pass," and so he is able to continue on. But when we gain some success or happiness, which is also the result of past activity, we find it more difficult to be equipoised because we are attached to our success and want to think that it is ours. The great devotee Queen Kunti therefore prayed to the Lord to let calamities befall her again and again because she would then see Him again and again, and by seeing the Lord constantly she would never see repeated birth and death. Simply by thinking of Krishna, our difficulties turn into occasions for realizing Krishna's mercy.

There is another time of tolerance, a more difficult time of testing in which the Lord apparently withdraws His divine mercy and the devotee feels himself alone and helpless. Perhaps this is due to some offense committed knowingly or unknowingly, or it may simply arise from the Lord's desire to increase the hankering of the devotee for Him. It is certainly not the position of the devotee to question his Lord or to demand anything from Him, not even an acknowledgement of service or explanation of His ways. Still, if a devotee is faithful and perseveres without doubting—in other words, if he is tolerant—the sunlight of Krishna consciousness will surely dawn in his soul very soon. Krishna has promised never to leave us alone, never to forsake us. We must rest assured that His word can never fail.

☆☆☆☆☆☆☆☆☆☆☆☆☆☆

Meditation 35

Satisfaction Through Service

"THE THOUGHTS OF My pure devotees dwell in Me, their lives are surrendered to Me, and they derive great satisfaction and bliss enlightening one another and conversing about Me." (*Bhagavad-gita* 10:9)

The standard of material happiness revolves around leisure and opulence. The great demon Hiranyakasipu was so named because of his attraction for soft beds and gold, which are still the most important things in most people's lives. Everyone wants to enjoy life. As long as the checks keep coming, who objects if there is no work? Because people identify themselves with the body rather than with the soul, they want to gratify the senses more and more. That is the only standard of happiness a materialist knows. But a devotee simply wants to serve Krishna, whether there is pay or not. A pure devotee does not pray for wealth or fame, nor for his daily bread. He prays only for causeless devotional service birth after birth. He does not want anything for himself.

We must therefore desire service rather than comfort if we want to attract the attention of Krishna. We must shun the fleeting pleasures of the senses in order to enjoy the eternal bliss of the spirit.

Yet there are many obstacles and temptations that may prevent our attaining such a lofty goal. Attachment to the mind and the misuse of freedom—common faults in us all—result in pride and selfishness, which degrade the soul. God certainly wants to give us His blessings, for He is the Friend and Well-wisher of all, but unfortunately we do not know how to take His gifts. Indeed, God is always giving us something—the sun, the rain, food, knowledge from holy books and holy men—but how we use them is the important question. If we want perfect results, we have to use God's gifts perfectly, according to His direction.

Sometimes we use God's gifts but show no gratitude. Then too, we are barred from divine grace. What happiness can there be in obeying God simply out of fear that if we don't, we'll go to hell? Real happiness begins when we take pleasure in the privilege of being able to serve Him. God is so kind: He has given us life, intelligence, the power of speech, an eye for beauty, and an ear for hearing transcendental sound vibration. If we are grateful, how do we show it?

First of all, we must stop trying to make God our order supplier. We should stop being so concerned with being saved ourselves and should be more concerned with saving others by engaging them in devotional service. We should give the knowledge of devotional service freely and not worry about becoming a big devotee. We should remember that not everything big is great, not everything high is holy. Not all that tastes sweet is always for our good, and not all desires are pure. Things pleasant to us are not always pleasing to God. Let us become humble and contrite, ready to accept every difficulty He sends as necessary for His service. Then we may begin to know the meaning of eternal love.

Everyone is anxious to receive something from God, but who is anxious to give to God? Materialists are always out to get, to acquire, to amass, to conquer, to subjugate, to rule, to enjoy, to lord it over all they survey. Only the devotee wants to serve. By serving God first, we inclusively serve man, animals, plants, the earth. We are forever servants, eternal servants of God and of everything else as part of Him. This is the universal vision that brings peace. How can there be peace for those who want to possess what is not rightly theirs? It is only life at the basest level, the level of beasts, that exists by grabbing. The life of the spirit fulfills itself by giving. Man's glory is not in conquering space or in lording it over material resources but in distributing Krishna consciousness to all. Therefore, the Vedas prescribe sacrifice, charity, and penance. These activities in the mode of goodness are as natural to the enlightened man as the hard struggle for existence is to animals and materialistic men.

Thus, we should ever strive to learn from the gifts of God how to give rightly to others. All good things come from Him and not from ourselves. One who forgets this suffers separation from Him. Let us give Him all credit for what is right and true, and blame ourselves alone for deficiencies and negligence. God is the greatest, and next to Him we are nothing. Let us therefore take the low seat, that He may raise us up. The saints most esteemed are those who thought themselves the least. The great Bhaktivinode Thakur saw himself as "a wicked materialist, always addicted to worldly desires," with "no good qualities." The more we humble ourselves, the more glorious God makes us. The more we eschew the false glory of this world, the more we become filled with truth and beauty. The more we feel our own helplessness, the greater the strength we get from Him. By seeking only His pleasure and satisfaction, and always describing His glories to others, we will find the greatest happiness and contentment.

☆☆☆☆☆☆☆☆☆☆☆☆☆☆

Meditation 36

Selfless Service

"THE SUPREME OCCUPATION [*dharma*] for all humanity is that by which men can attain to loving devotional service unto the transcendent Lord. Such service must be unmotivated and uninterrupted in order to completely satisfy the self." (*Srimad-Bhagavatam* 1:2:6)

We work gladly when there are great stakes involved, but few want to serve only for the service. Many approach God in times of distress, or for some material benediction, or out of curiosity, but few draw near simply to know and love Him. It is easy to pray devoutly, "Dear God, please help me out of this difficulty," or, "Please, dear Lord, just give me this or that and I will be Your good servant." But few are ready to petition, "O Almighty Lord, I have no desire to accumulate wealth, nor do I desire beautiful women, nor do I want any number of followers. I want only Your causeless devotional service birth after birth." (*Sikshastaka* 4) Many are willing to follow the path when it is smooth and easy, but few can say, "I know no one but Krishna as my Lord, and He shall remain so even if He handles me roughly by His embrace or makes me brokenhearted by not being present before me. He is completely free to do anything and everything, for He is always my worshipful Lord, unconditionally." (*Sikshastaka* 8) What transcendental power there is in pure, unmotivated surrender!

Prahlad Maharaj said that those who serve to get some benediction from the Lord are no different from businessmen. Does not their calculation of profit and loss mean that they love themselves more than God? Devotees of the caliber of Prahlad, however, never want anything for themselves. They want only to serve the Lord according to His desires. Such devotees are very, very rare, and also very, very dear to Krishna.

Giving all one's wealth in charity, performing great austerities and penances, cultivating transcendental knowledge, and following the regulative principles cannot compare to pure devotional service. Two points are especially noteworthy in this verse: that this service is not only unmotivated but also uninterrupted. There is a class of so-called devotees who think that devotional service is a good way to rapidly attain higher consciousness. But then they think that they will give up serving and become the Supreme Enjoyer, God. If motivated service denotes a business attitude, this mentality is that of a murderer: serve God to become strong, and then kill Him and become God yourself. The Kingdom of God, however, is never taken by force, nor can God's position ever be usurped.

If we want to conquer God, we must learn the art from the *gopis* of Vrindaban. Krishna is never defeated by weapons and armies but by the love of His devotees. Indeed, He told the *gopis* that it was impossible to repay them or show gratitude for their love. He who could not be defeated by all the kings of the earth was conquered by the milkmaids of Vrindaban. Therefore, Lord Chaitanya advises us to follow the *gopis'* example through the process of pure devotional service, for Krishna is easily attained by a fully surrendered soul.

Finally, we should note that such service is completely satisfying to the self. Materialists wonder how it is possible for devotees to give up illicit sex, intoxication, meat eating, and gambling. "What do you do for fun?" they ask. "Serve God," we reply. Do you not know, O foolish men, that Krishna is the reservoir of all pleasure, and that serving Him is like diving into the ocean of nectar? Lord Krishna's devotees are not fools. We have not given up something for nothing, but something base for something sublime. We have left something temporal for that which is eternal. Who would not exchange a life of misery—birth, old age, disease, and death—for one that is eternal, full of knowledge and bliss? Is it really a great austerity to give up eating cold leftovers when offered mountains of delicious sweetmeats?

To become the servant of God is no ordinary thing. Just as the servant of a king lives almost on the same level with the king, the servant of God lives always with God, and he is honored as much as God because of his being the most confidential servant of God. Still, he thinks himself the most fallen, unprofitable servant of the servant. Indeed, his humility, even in the face of wealth and adoration, is his greatest asset. He calls himself weak, but he is more powerful than the entire material energy; he calls himself poor, but he possesses the greatest wealth in love of God; he calls himself servant, but he is fit to be Prabhupada, master of all.

☆☆☆☆☆☆☆☆☆☆☆☆☆☆☆☆

Meditation 37

Pitfalls On The Path

"ONE'S DEVOTIONAL SERVICE is spoiled when he becomes too entangled in the following six activities: 1) eating more than necessary or collecting more funds than required; 2) overendeavoring for mundane things that are very difficult to obtain; 3) talking unnecessarily about mundane subject matters; 4) practicing the scriptural rules and regulations only for the sake of following them and not for the sake of spiritual advancement, or rejecting the rules and regulations of the scriptures and working independently or whimsically; 5) associating with worldly-minded persons who are not interested in Krishna consciousness; and 6) being greedy for mundane achievements." (*Nectar of Instruction*)

Devotional service is the one sure and easy process to attain Krishna consciousness, but there are many pitfalls that can hinder our progress if we are not careful. Here, Rupa Goswami lists six pitfalls, foremost of which is the tendency to accept too much: too much food, too much clothing, too much comfort, even too much facility for service. It is a great virtue to know when one has enough. One who is not satisfied with the bare necessities of life can never be satisfied with more. Therefore, we should be content with what is easily obtained and actually needed.

Although human life is meant for plain living and high thinking, modern material civilization aims at high living and not much thinking, and thus paves the way for repeated birth and death in the lower species of life. Those who are serious about making spiritual progress, therefore, are advised to avoid excessive comforts for the physical body. Living simply here and now means having a better chance to secure spiritual treasures in the life hereafter. Even the animals do not waste their time with hard endeavor for the necessities of life, but by nature's arrangement, they eat and sleep quite well. Why does only man have an economic problem? Is it not because he has forgotten the plan of his Creator? To become a harmonious part of the whole, we have only to realize that God has made all things perfect and complete.

Unnecessary talk for mundane purposes has been likened to the croaking of a frog. When the frog loudly croaks, he reveals his whereabouts to the snake, who quickly comes and devours him. Similarly, when we engage in idle chatter, we call *maya*, the illusory energy, to come and cover us in forgetfulness of Krishna. Not only talking, but watching television, playing cards, needless exercising, and frivolous sports are also useless activities. They cause us to neglect our real duty of serving God, to miss our valuable opportunity for Krishna consciousness, and to glide down the merry road to hell. Of course, talks about God and devotional service are not discouraged, for such talks are always beneficial and most enjoyable.

Spiritual discipline is meant for ultimate liberation. Those who want to use the spiritual science for material purposes and those who neglect the authorized process are both condemned herein. We should not try to use God for our own selfish purposes but give our lives as a living sacrifice in His service. Nothing material that can be used in devotional service should be neglected, nor should we concoct religious principles according to our fancy. Mental speculators and whimsical innovators are simply a disturbance to the society of bona fide devotees.

The association of pure devotees increases our love of God, while the association of those addicted to the pleasures of this life causes us to forget God. Association with impersonalist philosophers encourages one to think, "I am God," and thus one loses his chance to engage in ever blissful service to God. An intelligent devotee, avoids all these different kinds of materialists and thus proceeds straight on the path to love of God.

The final danger is akin to the first: being greedy for mundane achievements. Both individually and collectively, we want to accumulate more and more, and this is the cause of all our problems in the world. God is the actual Proprietor of everything because only He is its Creator, Maintainer, and Destroyer. Everything rests upon His supreme will, for everything emanates from Him alone. If we want peace and prosperity, we have to cultivate the quality of surrender and avoid things that destroy our devotional sentiment. This alone can bring peace. The best practice is to chant the Holy Names of God constantly. Hare Krishna!

☆☆☆☆☆☆☆☆☆☆☆☆☆☆☆☆

Meditation 38

Making Devotional Service Easy

"THERE ARE SIX principles favorable to the execution of pure devotional service: 1) being enthusiastic, 2) endeavoring with confidence, 3) being patient, 4) acting according to regulative principles, 5) abandoning the association of nondevotees, and 6) following in the footsteps of the previous *acharyas*. These six principles undoubtedly assure the complete success of pure devotional service." (*Nectar of Instruction*, Text 3)

The shortest distance between two points is a straight line, and the quickest way to transcend is to be fixed in devotional service and never deviate from it. How unfortunate is the double-minded man, the one who tries to serve two masters! To try to kindle a fire while pouring water on it is surely frustrating. Just as there are many things detrimental to devotional service, there are many favorable, and if we are serious about advancing, we must continually adopt progressive means.

Of all factors, desire is the most important, and strong desire is expressed by enthusiasm. Even in material life, one is successful in proportion to his enthusiasm. But a materialist can be enthusiastic only as long as he is spurred on by the prospect of some gain, whereas a devotee remains enthusiastic even when there is great difficulty and suffering. To be zealous when all men defame you and to be fervent even when family and friends forsake you are qualifications for being the Lord's chosen vessel. Haridas Thakur loudly chanted the Holy Name, even after having been publicly beaten in twenty-two marketplaces. Such enthusiasm attracts the attention of Krishna.

Fanatics may also be enthusiastic, but their zeal is not well founded. With his consciousness rooted in Krishna, the Supreme Personality of Godhead, the devotee endeavors with great confidence and determination. No one is equal to God, and no one can surpass Him; therefore, if God be for us, who can be against us? Because the surrendered soul is fully protected by the promise of the Lord, he has unlimited faith by which he can easily move mountains or cross over the ocean of birth and death. Nor is that faith sentimental. It is proved again and again in the fire of adversity. He has no need to waste his life seeking greener pastures, or trying to adjust circumstances. Accepting whatever comes as the mercy of the Lord, the devotee passes his life peacefully and then enters into the Kingdom of God.

Whereas the frenzy of the materialist is soon dissipated, the hope of a devotee is perfected in patience. Patience is the symptom of complete surrender and is thus the greatest virtue, for it presages love of God. Patience means accepting hardship willingly for the Lord's sake and submissively waiting for His direction. To be answered "yes" or even "no" is not as difficult as being told to wait. But waiting for the Lord to reveal His will is just as much service as acting on His behalf. The devotee is perfect in patience by waiting for the Lord in all circumstances.

Thus we must courageously undertake the discipline of Krishna consciousness and execute the regulative principles of devotional service. Neglect of the regulative principles destroys our devotional enthusiasm. Beginning with hearing and chanting the name and fame of the Lord, we should increase our capacity to worship, serve, and remember Him at all times and in all places.

Remembering Him everywhere, however, does not give us license to associate with sinners in their sinful activity. Those who wait for God are never found in dens of iniquity. We can associate with non-devotees to give them Krishna consciousness, but not for sense gratification. This prohibition includes not only gross materialists and those of immoral character but also mental speculators, impersonalists desirous to become one with God, and bogus religionists who, seeking profit and adoration, refuse to surrender to God.

By strictly following in the footsteps of the pure devotees, we are sure to reach our desired goal. No guessing or theorizing is required, for we have only to understand the devotional principles from the bona fide spiritual master and execute them to our best ability. Then Krishna, who is the original Spiritual Master and the ability in us all, will manifest Himself to us and through us, and we will perfect our lives in His eternal love.

☆☆☆☆☆☆☆☆☆☆☆☆☆☆☆☆☆☆

PART TWO

Conversations With
The Lord In The Heart

Meditation 39

Awake, O Soul, To The Lord In The Heart

"I WORSHIP THE primeval Lord, Govinda, who is always seen by the devotee whose eyes are anointed with the pulp of love. He is seen in His eternal form of Shyamasundara situated within the heart of the devotee."—Lord Brahma *(Brahma-samhita 5:38)*

THE SOUL: Hear, O my soul, for He speaks to thee. Blessed is he who has ears to hear, and doubly blessed is he who hears the sound of His flute and feels the strong embrace of His arms. Blessed are they who catch the nectar emanating from His lotus mouth, and they who are no longer captivated by the whisperings of *maya*, however promising and alluring.

Thy word is Truth, and Truth is the greatest beauty. Who can compare to You, Thou handsome dark Youth, fairest of ten trillion? Blessed are the eyes smeared with the ointment of love, eyes that see You everywhere and everything in You and nothing apart from You. How wonderful are they who go beyond the senses to find You and to understand the transcendental mysteries of Your appearance and activities— Your Name, Your form, Your entourage, pastimes, and paraphernalia. Everything about You is Absolute in eternity, knowledge, and bliss.

Worshipable, too, are the great souls who have surrendered everything to Your Lotus Feet, leaving behind all of this world's grand illusions to enter into the reality of pure loving service to You.

Consider these things, dear soul, in the core of your heart and surrender utterly to Him. Engage all of your senses in the service of the Master of the senses, that they may be made whole in Him. How long you have been sleeping in forgetfulness! Wake up! Wake up! Listen to His voice, and to that of His external manifestation, the spiritual master, for they will guide you from without and within. Can't you hear Him now? "Shanti, shanti, peace, peace. Just surrender to Me, My child, and I will give you perfect protection."

Standing in His three-curved bending form, He bids us come and join in His eternal dance of love. Listen carefully: "I am the Life of all that lives. I am the Self seated in the hearts of all creatures. Indeed, I am in one sense everything, but I am independent. Whoever thinks always of Me becomes My devotee. He becomes a friend to Me, and I become a Friend to him. Whatever you do, do it for Me, and in this way you will surely come to Me. I promise you this, for you are very dear to Me."

Make haste, O friend! Dismiss the flickering cares and concerns of mortal life and join His band of loving slaves. What do you care for this temporal show when you can dance with Him, world-without-end? Do not hesitate or doubt. You ask, "What about wife and children, society and friends?"

"O foolish man," the sages reply, "which wife are you talking about? Whose children, what society and friends?" You have lived millions of lives, in millions of societies, with millions of fathers, mothers, sons, and daughters. They are all gone. Not even the names remain. Now you are free, free from obligations to forefathers or country or demigods or demons, for you have come to the final resting place—the Lotus Feet of the Lord. Rest well, O pilgrim, rest well. You have come home, never to leave again.

☆☆☆☆☆☆☆☆☆☆☆☆☆☆

Meditation 40

Please Be Visible To Me, O Lord

THE SOUL: Some have said that God cannot be seen, but You, O Lord of my heart, have said that by pure devotional service You can be seen in Your original, eternal form. Only to the foolish and envious are You hidden by Your creative potency, *maya*. They deride You, saying that You have no arms and legs nor feet nor hands, but it is they who are deficient because they have no eyes to see Your transcendental form of eternity, knowledge, and bliss. Your transcendental form moves more swiftly than the mind and is simultaneously visible and invisible. By Your own inconceivable potencies You are very, very near to Your devotee, but for others You are far, far away. Who can understand You? Who can comprehend Your ways? Only Your pure devotees can know Your infinite greatness in truth. Only they are qualified to give that knowledge to others.

Impersonalists, mental speculators, and even devotees who are not completely free from material desires resent approaching You through the medium of the spiritual master. Thinking that something is lost through an intermediary, they do not understand the miracle of discipular succession. What You spoke to Arjuna on the Battlefield of Kurukshetra is not different from what is spoken by Your representative today.

Indeed, the divine vibration becomes sweeter by being carefully passed on from one spiritual master to another. It is just like a mango that, being high on a tree, is allowed to fully ripen in the sun and is then handed down from one person to another until it reaches the ground, perfectly intact. You are the real Guru, the source of all knowledge, and You manifest Yourself externally and internally so that we can know You as You are. Therefore, I do not think that there is any difference between hearing from my guru and hearing directly from You. Both are You, both are full knowledge and perfect Truth. Both are competent to take me back home, back to Godhead.

Therefore, let me take the dust of the lotus feet of my spiritual master on my head again and again, for it is by the mercy of the pure devotee that one obtains Your mercy. One cannot know the Absolute Truth simply by observing celibacy, strictly following the rules and regulations of household life, living as a mendicant, or even undergoing severe penances and austerities. The Absolute Truth is revealed only to one who has attained the mercy of Your pure devotee.

You are the Supersoul in everyone's heart, and from You come knowledge, remembrance, and forgetfulness. To those who surrender to You, You give knowledge from without and remembrance from within; and for those who are envious of You, You grant forgetfulness, by which they can imagine themselves to be God, or whomever else they want to be. But to me, You are the only transcendent reality, the Cause of all causes, the source of all manifestations, by whom all these universes are maintained, and in whom they come to rest. You are the eternally effulgent Lord, directly and indirectly conscious of all and yet aloof from all. You are the reality of all things. It is only due to Your influence that unreal things, such as this phenomenal world, appear real. You are the Absolute Truth, eternally existent in Your transcendental abode, forever perfect and complete. Let me meditate upon You, O Govinda, for You are the Lord of my life.

☆☆☆☆☆☆☆☆☆☆☆☆☆☆☆

Meditation 41

Relish His Messages

THE SOUL: O Lord of my heart, let me hear Your messages of eternal love, for they are sweeter than honey and more valuable than gems and pearls. In wisdom and knowledge they surpass the profanity of all philosophers and speculators of mundane fame. They are virtuous in themselves and not tainted by human understanding. For receiving them, there is no qualification, save the childlike ability to hear and believe.

THE LORD IN THE HEART: Originally I spoke these sayings to Brahma, Narada, and Vyas, and I repeat them to you today because you are My surrendered soul, and you have developed unalloyed love for Me. To one who sincerely asks, I give My Supreme Word. From within I am the still, small voice of Supersoul, and from without, I am the voice of the spiritual master. Through all different species of life I accompany you, directing your wanderings, witnessing your activities, and giving you a chance to become free from misery and distress. Unfortunately, you were deaf to My instruction, listening to the promises of *maya* and preferring the temporary gratification of your senses to the transcendental pleasure of God. How foolish you were! What can men, demigods, or demons offer but the bedazzling sensations of material intoxication, which are here today and gone tomorrow? Yet, rascals and fools diligently serve *maya* in a hard struggle for existence. Though they reap little profit, they still refuse to serve Me, the Soul of their very self. Only I can give them an eternal life of knowledge and bliss, but because they envy Me, their eyes are covered by My deluding potency and they cannot see Me as I am.

How complete is the illusion created by My *maya*! For the slightest chance of gain, men travel to the ends of the earth, but for going back home, back to Godhead, they hardly lift a foot. They work like asses, live like rats, scrap like cats and dogs, and spend their whole life fighting in court for some insignificant pieces of paper; but for a reward beyond calculation and estimate, for the greatest good and honor, and for God's glory and their own peace of mind, they have no time. It is to their eternal shame that they begrudge their Creator, Maintainer, and Friend—the Supreme Personality of Godhead—His rightful due. O, you unprofitable servants! What will become of you at the judgement court of Death, when you are called to give an account of your every breath?

The promises of *maya* are always false, but My promises never fail. Nor does anyone go away empty-handed who surrenders to Me. I have given My word: "For My devotee, I preserve what he has and supply what he lacks." I will surely give what I have promised. Even a mundane good man keeps his word. How can the Supreme Good not fulfill His vow? O ye of little faith! If only you remain faithful and serve Me with all your heart, developing pure love for Me alone, I, who am the rewarder of all those who diligently seek Me, will come and be a Friend to you, and you will be a friend to Me.

Listen again to my instruction: Meditate upon Me, become My devotee, chant My Holy Name, and always ponder my words in your heart so that you may never forget Me. Thus I will always live with you and direct your every action. Do not fear temptation and testing, for I am there also, and am able to make all things work for the good and glory of My devotee. By such dealings I purify your imperfections and increase your love for Me. My devotee will never perish, and his perfection is guaranteed.

THE SOUL: My dear Lord Krishna, sustainer of all that be, You are the all good Supreme Personality of Godhead. How can I know You, or approach You, or speak to You? I am not at all worthy. Only by the causeless mercy of Your external manifestation, the spiritual master, do I directly realize and perceive You, the Absolute Truth. Who can fathom Your divine grace when I, the poorest and meanest of servants, not as useful as a worm in stool, have been numbered among Your eternal loving servants? My actual position is so vile that if a pious man even thinks of me, he loses all his pious credits. Still, You have remembered me and sent Your confidential representative to rescue me. I am nothing. I possess nothing. There is nothing I can do for You, who are complete in Yourself, possessing all opulences—wealth, fame, beauty, knowledge, strength, and renunciation—simultaneously and to an unlimited degree. You alone are all good and kind. You are the expert Mystic, and You can do all things as You desire. Therefore, my dear Lord, kindly fulfill the desire of Your most insignificant servant and allow me to engage eternally in Your loving service. Please, O Master, do not hide Your face from me or make me brokenhearted by not being present before me, lest I become like a barren desert or a severed hand. Break me, smash me, do what You want to teach me to surrender to Your divine will, but do not deprive me of the service of Your Lotus Feet.

☆☆☆☆☆☆☆☆☆☆☆☆☆☆☆☆

Meditation 42

Knowledge Culminates In Surrender

THE LORD IN THE HEART: My dear friend, how long will you ignore Me and fail to recognize your very Self? Listen to Me, and learn of your true nature. You are a part of Me, and with Me you can never fall down. Only when you forget Me, and rebel against My sovereignty, do you fall under the influence of My illusory energy.

THE SOUL: O Lord, I want to surrender to You, but it seems impossible. Because I am always identifying myself with this body and mind, I am subject to the many illusions of material desires. My eternal enemy, lust, gives me no rest, and I am always afflicted with anger. Unless You help me, I have no hope.

THE LORD IN THE HEART: Gladly do I teach you, My friend, for we are eternal companions. Through millions of lives we have traveled together. I remember them all, but you cannot. Only when you become free from all material contamination can you have perfect knowledge. Listen again to My supreme instruction, which is for your benefit.

Never was there a time when I did not exist, nor you, nor all others. But those who want My association must walk in the light. Men walk in darkness because their deeds are evil. Nor do they want to be corrected. Consider your ways, dear soul. Are they of My direction, or of the illusory desire for sense pleasure? In ignorance you misidentify yourself with your material senses and thereby lose the spiritual awareness by which you can experience the limitless bliss of the Absolute. Give up such ignorance, and with great determination and remorse, forsake your false dreams. Walk with Me in the beauty of virtue. Be perfect, but never think yourself to be meritorious for your good works. Knowing that every good and perfect thing comes from Me, never consider yourself to be the doer or the enjoyer of anything. Man proposes; God disposes.

Due to vain imagination, you have become a great offender. You have rebelled against My authority and usurped My property. Imagining yourself to be God, the lord of all you survey, you are filled with the modes of passion and ignorance and cannot accomplish anything of value. You fall easily and are easily defeated, always disturbed, and unsteady. In you there is no good thing, but there are many things that are vile. You are also as helpless as a newborn child. Therefore, you should not feel proud of anything, nor glory in anything that is not spiritual, for all flesh is as grass, which today is and tomorrow is cut down and cast into the fire. Consider nothing to be important or worthwhile, save that which is eternal, and let My Truth be your only joy. Do not fear anything, nor shun anything that is favorable for My service, but flee from evil, especially lust.

Some men profess to worship Me, but their hearts are far from Me. Out of vanity, arrogance, pride, and lust, they try to exploit My energies for the gratification of their senses, but they are doomed to bewilderment and frustration. Material nature works under My direction, helping those who sincerely seek Me and confusing those who oppose Me. Equal to all, I fulfill the desires of everyone. Therefore, O soul, be careful to desire that which is best and highest of all—love of God.

Not everyone who claims to be My devotee is actually so, not even everyone who chants My Holy Name. But one who follows My instructions and those of My pure devotee is indeed My devotee. Devotion is not necessarily acquired from universities and books, nor from pictures, nor even from worshiping My transcendental form. Purified senses and genuine surrender are required. My devotees constantly long for Me and converse about My transcendental activities. Reluctantly do they hear or speak of anything material; indeed, they frequently neglect the necessities of their own bodies. In all their actions they consider My satisfaction, not caring for their own future, either in heaven or hell. Such devotees are very, very rarely found in this world. If one is so fortunate as to come in contact with one such pure devotee for even a moment, his life immediately becomes successful. Very soon he returns to My abode, never to leave again.

☆☆☆☆☆☆☆☆☆☆☆☆☆☆

Meditation 43

Learn To Love Purely

THE SOUL: O Lord of my heart, blessed is Your Holy Name, and blessed am I that You condescend to live with me, although I am the least of all creatures. May I remain ever aware of You, to serve You in pure devotion.

O sweet Lord, my Beloved, when I think of You, my whole being rejoices, and when I feel Your presence, I feel like the springtime earth awakening from a long winter's sleep. You enliven my senses to perceive You everywhere.

How kind You are! Even in tribulation and death, You remain near,

O my hope and refuge. But my love is yet weak and tender, like a newly sprouted creeper. Protect me, my Lord, and nurture me to perfection. Keep me from unholy pleasures and make me ever aware of the pleasure of devotion to You. Purify my heart of all affections save those related to You or to things connected to You. Make my love perfect, even as Your love is perfect.

THE LORD IN THE HEART: My dear little soul, you have spoken wisely. Now hear from Me of the ways of eternal love.

Love is the most excellent state of being and the greatest virtue for all who possess it. It makes difficult things easy and tolerates injustices with equanimity. The burdens of love are light, and all its dealings are like nectar and honey. Such wondrous loving exchanges I display in My pastimes of love with Radha in Vrindaban, or in the madness of separation from Sita when She is kidnapped by the demon Ravana. You should know that since My love is never material, it can never be compared to the feelings of ordinary boys and girls, who are simply playthings in the hands of lust. My love always tends upward and is irresistible, like the force of the sea, inexorably pulling everything back to Me. It cannot be checked by any power.

I advise you, My child, to make your love for Me exclusive. You cannot have two lovers. You will either love the first and despise the second, or you will be faithful to the second and misuse the first. You cannot love Me and love the world; therefore, give up all worldly affections and love Me alone, lest your inward vision again become blurred and your determination to achieve Me slacken.

Nothing can be sweeter than love, nor mightier, nor more pervasive, nor more ecstatic, nor more to be desired in all three worlds. Love emanates from Me and rests in Me, and the joy of those who possess it knows no bounds. In jubilation they run, jump, and laugh like madmen, not caring about outsiders or time and place. Love gives all and verily gains all.

Because it reflects the limitless, love knows no limit. Love is fearless, undaunted, bold, and daring. For the satisfaction of the beloved, it attempts more than is possible, and considers nothing impossible.

For this reason, love performs and accomplishes more than this world can dream of.

This eternal love of which I speak is ever alert. It rests, but does not sleep; it wearies, but does not tire. In perplexing situations, it remains calm. Like the great Himalayas, it is immovable. It is swifter than the mind, refreshing like the nighttime dew, pleasant like the morning sun, kind like a true friend, patient like an ascetic, faithful like a good husband, and prudent like a sage. Love never seeks its own interest, for such business dealings transform love into lust. Having full faith in the beloved, love tolerates every difficult and distasteful thing. Indeed, suffering is the proof of true love, for never was there love without pain. Thus one who cannot endure all things for the pleasure of the beloved is not worthy of the name of lover.

THE SOUL: Do not only speak of this love, O Krishna, but grant me a double portion, I pray. O My Lord, my Beloved, be mine, even as I am Yours. Increase my love that I may constantly hear Your flute calling me to the holy land of Vraja, where I can know Your transcendental pastimes of love. Who witnesses the wonders of Your transcendental sport? Who tastes the sweetness of Your lips and feels the strong embrace of Your powerful arms? Only by pure devotional service can You be known as You are.

O Krishna, Your transcendental form exudes a fragrance that shames both the rose and jasmine. How soothing is Your love! How blissful to bask and bathe in it!

O Krishna, where have You gone? Where are You now? Why do You hide from me? Let me ask the trees and flowers. Can anyone tell me where Krishna has gone? O Krishna, please answer me. I want to end this nightmare existence of Your absence. I long to rise above the limited conception of self and enter into the all-blissful realization of being Your eternal loving slave. Therefore, let me sing my song of love, O Govinda, and follow You wherever You go. Let me leave this body now, while I am chanting Your Holy Name: Krishna, Krishna, Krishna.

☆☆☆☆☆☆☆☆☆☆☆☆☆☆

Meditation 44

Constancy In Love

THE LORD IN THE HEART: My dear little child, do not think that you are already a bold and perfect lover.

THE SOUL: Why not, my Lord?

THE LORD IN THE HEART: Because a first class lover is constant in all circumstances and makes no demands, whereas you, My dear child, give up your duty when there is a slight difficulty. Besides, you are too desirous of consolation.

The pure lover is steady in both happiness and distress and is unmoved by the allurements of sense pleasure, however attractive they may appear. A true lover is satisfied equally in good times and bad, in sickness and health, in poverty and plenty. He is equally pleased with whatever his beloved gives, regarding the love of the giver more than the gift of the lover. Even if one can offer Me only a leaf, a flower, a little fruit, or some water, I am completely satisfied if he does so with great affection. The perfect lover, then, is not concerned with rewards but with Me alone, for I am the source of every good and perfect gift.

Your love is also imperfect because you are attached to feelings of ecstasy and devout fervor, which are sometimes present and sometimes withdrawn. Experiencing great enthusiasm and excitement in your service from time to time is not as important as being fixed in that service. Pleasant and exhilarating emotions that come and go may sometimes be a gift of special mercy to encourage a neophyte lover in My service, or they may arise from the modes of material nature or the action of the mind, which is always accepting and rejecting according to its flickering desires. You may accept such mercy as a foretaste of your eternal, blissful Krishna consciousness, but do not be attached to it, lest it become another material hankering for personal gratification. Be attached only to Me and My service. Then you will be ready to fight the good fight against the illusory energy, *maya*, which tries to hide Me from you. Subdue evil thoughts, shun the passion for pleasure, avoid unholy association, and always think of Me. These are the characteristics of My pure lovers.

Why do you consider temptation a sign of My displeasure? Quite the contrary, temptations prove and glorify My devotee, showing him to be greater than all the forces of illusion. In your struggle and determined fight, you prove your love for Me and earn great merit, but never slacken your attention nor lower your guard against the wiles of *maya*. Like a jealous lover, *maya* will do all in her power to hinder your service and dampen your resolve to serve Me. *Maya* flings her arrows of doubt to distract you and fills your mind with thoughts of sense gratification to bewilder and weaken you. Then you neglect to chant My Holy Name and to hear of My eternal pastimes and activities from My pure devotees. Consequently your love becomes cold and lifeless, and you fall down to enjoy with lovers of material life.

Do not believe or even listen to the voice of *maya*, whose only purpose is to deceive you and divert your service away from Me and toward herself. Take My strength by chanting My Name: Hare Krishna, Hare Krishna. As I have protected so many in the past, I will also protect you. But you must want Me and My help more than anything else. Do not be afraid to cry for Me. I am very moved by the tears of a sincere devotee who calls out in great desperation. Give up attachment even to life itself and prefer to die rather than surrender to *maya*, though she may promise you the whole world. After all, the world lasts for only a season, but My pleasures are forever.

Take heart, dear little one. I am not far away. I am very, very near to those who sincerely seek Me, and I have promised to give them shelter from every harm. Therefore, fight like a valiant warrior, and if you sometimes fall—either from weakness, accident, or the expertise of your enemy—do not be discouraged. Stand up and fight again with renewed strength and vigor, knowing that I am with you and will surely give you victory in the end. But beware of false pride. Victory will come not from your side but from Mine. You can be but an instrument in the fight. If you think that you can defeat the enemy alone, you are doomed. Since many have already fallen, let their destruction be a warning to you. Just depend on Me, and not on yourself. Use wisely the strength and weapons that I give you, and you will triumph by My grace. Now, my dear child, rise and fight. Victory awaits you.

☆☆☆☆☆☆☆☆☆☆☆☆☆☆☆☆☆

Meditation 45

Ecstatic Love Goes Well With Humility

THE LORD IN THE HEART: Why do you pride yourself on your material body, the land of your birth, or the good qualities awarded by the grace of God? Even your spiritual advancement is My gift, and not your own doing. Therefore, humble yourself before Me, bow down to

Me, and thank Me for My favor, lest it be taken away and given to another more worthy. Take more pleasure in My ministry than in My praise, and be more attached to serving My servants than to feeling ecstatic emotions that come and go. When you are experiencing great love and devotional fervor, remember how empty your life was without Me. Your advancement in Krishna consciousness does not depend on ecstatic feelings but on your being fixed in My service in all circumstances. When these feelings of love are absent, know that it is the symptom of genuine affection to continue with humility and patience in the performance of your duties, always remembering that it is for Me that you work.

My ways are far above yours. Do not try to understand the mind of God, for you are a most insignificant creature. Nor are you the controller of your own destiny. Everything is dependent on My will. I know what is desired by every living entity; therefore to one person I give the grace of divine knowledge, and from another I withdraw it. I am the Friend and Well-wisher of all, but not all feel the same for Me. Many become lazy and impatient with Me when things do not go as they desire. I know them better than they know themselves, and I give what is best. Why do they not trust Me?

Others carelessly use My divine gifts, not appreciating their infinite value, and waste their precious human life in living like animals—simply eating, sleeping, defending, and mating. Or, due to being puffed up with their own importance, they imagine that they can do more than I empower them to. Thus, failing to consider their own frailty, they fall victim to the sin of pride. Be completely dependent on Me. With My help, even though you attempt the impossible, your labor will not go in vain.

The snares on the path of transcendental love are unknown to the inexperienced and neophyte lover, who may easily fall prey to the adversary unless guided by My expert lovers, My pure devotees. Unfortunately, the neophyte, failing to know My real desires, often wishes to follow his own concocted opinions. Just try to understand Me from My pure devotee, the bona fide spiritual master, for he is the most confidential lover of all. Give up your vanity and learn from him. He is very kind and anxious to help. Be not wise in your own estimation, lest you make yourself a fool. A little knowledge is a dangerous thing when devoid of Me, whereas a small quantity of true learning humbly acquired with understanding of Me is equal to all the treasures of My Kingdom. Therefore, it may be better that you be poor, destitute, or uneducated and attain My favor than opulent and suffer My separation due to pride.

Blessed are the humble, for they can feelingly chant My Holy Name. If you would be wise, remain insignificant in your own eyes. Then you will be esteemed by all. Give up the spirit of enjoyment, and you will learn to rule the restless senses and avoid misdeeds. Be brave in adversity, and think confidently of Me.

If you are feeling blissful in My love, resolve to act no differently when the bliss subsides, and have faith that it will return when I wish. Even the great saint Narada was told that he could not perpetually relish the ecstasy of My presence until he was fully purified from all material contamination. Such tribulations and disappointments are ultimately for your benefit, more so than what you yourself might desire. A soul's merit is measured not by ecstatic trance, nor by ability to recite scriptures, nor by mystic powers, nor by authority over others, but by the devotee's surrender to Me and the humility with which he walks in My ways. The great soul is he who always chants My glories and endeavors with great determination to carry out My orders for the welfare of all. Such a one is very, very dear to Me and abides with me always.

☆☆☆☆☆☆☆☆☆☆☆☆☆☆☆☆☆

Meditation 46

Hoping Against Hope

THE SOUL: Dear Lord Krishna, I, who am but one ten-thousandth the size of the tip of a hair, the most minute atom of Your infinite being, prostrate myself before You again and again. Being so small and weak, I am always falling under the control of Your external energy, imagining myself to be something other than Your eternal servant and thereby identifying my pure spiritual being with temporary, abominable matter. This causes me unlimited suffering. Thinking that I am this body I now inhabit, I become very attached to it. Indeed, I imagine it to be very beautiful and wonderful, although it is nothing but a lump of rotting flesh. Without the presence of the soul, the body cannot live, move, love, or even have consciousness. Although stupid, I think that I am intelligent. Although all greatness and power are Yours, in illusion I think that I am the great and powerful. Fool that I am, I do not even know my real identity, nor why I am here.

It is Your causeless mercy alone, manifested through Your pure devotees, that can overcome this ignorance and light up my darkened heart with the torchlight of knowledge. In the brightness of Krishna consciousness, all my illusions are dispelled, and I can see things as they are—past, present, and future. With infinite grace, You enlighten me about my own true nature: Your eternal part and parcel, Your eternal servant. Without You I am nothing; empowered by You I can do anything. Leaning on Your strong arms and uplifted and supported by You, I am filled with unspeakable joy, but when I think myself independent and self-sufficient, I am always miserable and full of anxiety and remorse.

It is only Your eternal love that can save me. I can do nothing, nor claim any credit. I cannot even sustain my life or protect myself from the smallest dangers. You supply all my needs and guard me from every evil, more than I can perceive or know. Indeed, whatever evil I encounter is simply due to my failing to take shelter of You, thinking that I know better than You what is good for me. What a great fool I am! Not realizing that You are the Soul of my soul, I do not understand that by loving You, I will satisfy both You and myself simultaneously. In giving up something false and useless, I will gain a priceless gem, for You, dear Krishna, give Yourself to the surrendered soul, a gift beyond imagination, calculation, or hope.

What can a wretch like me add to Your glory? Can a mosquito augment the magnificence of an elephant? Even if he rides on the elephant, can he brag that he is an intimate associate of the elephant? If anything, he is a disturbance. Therefore, my sweet Lord, let Your own great munificence be Your glory, and let Your infinite loving kindness be Your praise. Although I am not worthy of even Your notice, You have displayed the beauty of Your condescension by making me Your eternal servant. Out of Your great nobility and compassion, You never cease to favor me and also chastise me, although I am ungrateful and unsubmissive.

I therefore pray, My Lord, that You correct my rebellious mentality and make me a truly profitable servant—thankful, humble, and devout. Teach me to chant Your Holy Name with faith and gratitude. You have made Yourself easily available in the sound of Your Name, but I am most unfortunate: I have no attraction for it. Help me, O God. Without Your help, I have no hope.

✫✫✫✫✫✫✫✫✫✫✫✫✫✫✫

Meditation 47

God Is The Source Of All Value

THE LORD IN THE HEART: My little one, I am the beginning, the middle, and the end of all beings. If you want to be blessed, you must make Me your only goal, for without connection to Me, nothing has any reality. Therefore, at the time of creation I proclaimed, "O Brahma, whatever appears to be of value actually has no reality if it is without relation to Me. Know it as My illusory energy, the reflection that appears in darkness." How can you be happy if you perversely love what is illusory? If you concentrate all your affections in Me, My child, you will purify your existence and attain to My abode. Why do men neglect My service, preferring the service of their insatiable senses, for which they receive no profit, but endure great frustration? Their hearts become dry and hard like stone, and I cannot live there.

I am the source of both the material and spiritual worlds, for everythings rests upon Me, like pearls on a thread. Therefore I advise you to relate all things to Me first, and then to others. Since others are but My infinitesimal parts, how can they have meaning without Me? When you understand how each and every thing relates to Me, the Origin of all, you will also comprehend its end in Me also. As water is given to the earth by the clouds and then returns again to the clouds through the rays of the sun, so everything that emanates from Me again returns to Me in due course of time.

It is from Me only that the rich and the poor, the great and the small draw the water of life. I am the Fountainhead of existence and the Root of being, and those who take My waters and return them again to Me, the Root of the tree of life, live perpetually in peace and happiness. They dwell always in My presence and know the smile of My face. But those who usurp My property for their own interests, who glory in their own pleasures, not caring for the sanction of the scriptures or the instructions of the holy teachers, live always in fear and torment, both in this life and hereafter.

My good and perfect ways work for the benefit of everyone. Do not ascribe any good to yourself or attribute holiness to man, because nothing can be good or holy without reference to Me, the all good Personality of Godhead. Men become good and holy when they surrender to Me, but without Me they are nothing. I have given all things for your use in My service, but with love and devotion they must be returned to Me. Whatever proceeds from Me must return to Me with thanksgiving. By this perfect knowledge, the wise put an end to all sinful reactions and thus avoid the repetition of birth and death.

Furthermore, you will thereby enter into the Vaikuntha atmosphere of heavenly grace and divine love, where neither envy nor selfishness nor smallness of heart nor the illusion of bodily love has any place. There, eternal love, pure love of God, pervades and envelops all, uniting all individual desires in My perfect complete whole.

Be wise, My child; think of Me constantly and rejoice in Me alone. Whatever you do, do for My satisfaction. Bow down to Me, offer fruits and flowers to Me, converse about Me, and chant My Holy Name. In this way you will come to Me without fail. I promise you this, for you are My very dear friend.

☆☆☆☆☆☆☆☆☆☆☆☆☆☆☆☆☆

Meditation 48

Serving God Brings Knowledge And Detachment

THE SOUL: Let me again speak, my Lord, for I cannot remain silent. My heart is filled with praise for Your causeless mercy upon me. Am I not the most wretched creature, deserving only Your wrath? Instead, You have lifted me out of the muck of material life and placed me as one of the atoms at Your Lotus Feet.

How sweet is Your service, my Lord! Who can know the nectar that You have reserved for those who dive into that great ocean of eternal love? Who can understand how You lovingly reciprocate with those who surrender everything to You? Contemplating that ecstasy of love dissolves my mortal bonds and makes me want to fly to You, O Lord of my life.

O high and great Lord, You are the sovereign of billions and trillions of Vaikuntha planets. Even the material nature works under Your direction. All the demigods bow down to You and worship You perpetually. Why do You condescend to accompany me through countless births in material existence? Why do You even bother with me? If one insignificant living entity out of an innumerable host is lost, what is that to You? From the pores of Your transcendental body flow numberless universes, each filled with unlimited beings generated with Your every breath.

My mind reels just thinking of Your infinity. Yet, You remember me. What munificence! What charity! Even though I have left Your eternal service to try to become a competitor god for my own sense enjoyment You have loved me and brought me back. Now, my God, I beg You never to let me forsake Your service or aspire for anything apart from You again. Be my Lord and Master eternally.

Unable to repay You for this favor, I shall remain forever indebted to You. O Fountainhead of unceasing love, Your pure devotional service is rarely achieved. There are many powerful mystic yogis, erudite scholars, learned philosophers, renounced sages, and ascetics who have given up all attachment to this mortal world; but a pure devotee of Your Lordship, a devotee who is completely free from mental speculation and fruitive activity, is very, very rare. You have shown unspeakable causeless mercy upon Your servant, beyond all hope, and You have displayed divine grace and friendship without consideration of merit.

How can I repay You for this special mercy? My service is but Your due, for it is the duty of every son to serve his father, and every servant his master. There is no recompense needed. Instead, I am the more indebted that You have stooped to engage one so poor and unworthy in Your loving service. Nor do I have anything to give You. Indeed, everything is already Yours including what I imagine to be mine and serve with. The material and spiritual worlds are fully under Your control, yet out of Your great love, You take pleasure in becoming the servant of Your pure devotee.

Then how shall I repay You? I know no way. What more can I do but beg to be Your menial slave birth after birth after birth? I don't want followers or wealth or women, but if I can just once render some pleasing service to You, my Lord, I will be satisfied. I am only an insignificant beggar, but You, O Lord of my heart, Lord of all, are worthy of perfect service, complete honor, and unending praise. This is our eternal relationship, and I wish it to remain so forever. Grant me this desire, I humbly pray.

☆☆☆☆☆☆☆☆☆☆☆☆☆☆☆☆

Meditation 49

Service Is Sweet, But Beware Of Overendeavor

THE SOUL: It is such a great honor to serve You, O Lord. The greatest pleasure results from renunciation for Your sake. Even austerities and penances, which appear very difficult to the worldly-minded, are great sources of joy and satisfaction for Your devotees. Seeing Your smiling face, or simply hearing "Well done, thou good and faithful servant," is sufficient reward to counteract all the miseries of material life.

O how sweet and consoling is Your service, purifying the mind and liberating the soul! Real freedom at last! To be free! Free from sin and free from shame, free from uncontrolled passion and worldly pride, free from the rat race of material life, and free from the repetition of birth and death. Free to love You completely, to become Your slave—yes, that is the highest liberation of all. In that bondage of love, I stand on the very ground of Divinity, where there is nothing more to be desired and nothing to be lost. Such a state, greater than all others, is pleasing to both God and man. It is the birthright of every being, the greatest good and most desirable goal. Its joy is without limit and its blessedness without end.

THE LORD IN THE HEART: You speak well, My child, but you have many things yet to understand.

THE SOUL: How can this be, my Lord? I have heard Your instructions for many years.

THE LORD IN THE HEART: That's all right. But still you do not know Me as I am. You do not even know my energies very minutely. Such knowledge is revealed only to those who are pure in heart and surrendered to Me in all their ways. You must conform totally to My desire, and dovetail all that you do to My will, for a lover with a separate interest is no lover at all. Desires different from Mine may excite you to great passion, but you should know whether you are acting for My pleasure or the pleasure of your senses. Attachment to results is indicative of self-interest, whereas contentment with whatever I ordain, realizing it to be My special mercy, is the sign of a pure devotee. Beware then of all desires that do not come from Me or My representative, the bona fide spiritual master. Although such desires may seem good and beneficial in the beginning, they will bear bitter fruit. Therefore, know My desire and what is truly good for you by reference to My word and to My pure devotee. Both are My external manifestations.

Do not be puffed up with your own ability to accomplish great things for Me, for even in My service one can overendeavor, thinking himself capable without My help. Better to carefully execute the instructions of My representative, the spiritual master, who knows the disciple through and through and knows best how to engage him in My service for his ultimate perfection. Rely on him and not on your own understanding, lest your mind become distracted and you again fall into *maya*. The enemy is most formidable, and sometimes you must forcibly control your passions. Don't even listen to the demands of the body, but feed the spirit with the transcendental sounds—My Holy Name and the narrations of My uncommon pastimes. The senses must be controlled with determination—even beaten, if need be, with the iron club of resolution. Let them remain in subjection continually, ready to satisfy Me in every way, wanting nothing in return. Take pleasure in plain living and high thinking, never complaining about bodily inconveniences. If you learn to tolerate every disturbance for My sake here and now, I will reward you abundantly in the life that is to come. Have faith in Me, My child. I shall surely bring it to pass.

☆☆☆☆☆☆☆☆☆☆☆☆☆☆☆

Meditation 50

Patience Is The Symptom Of Surrender

THE LORD IN THE HEART: Patience is another quality you must develop, in relation to material things as well as spiritual. Not only must you accept My desire unconditionally, but You must also wait patiently for Me to accomplish it.

THE SOUL: I can understand that patience is very important, my Lord, but why are there so many tribulations and so much adversity in my life? It seems that no matter what I plan to do, either for You or myself, I am not peaceful, nor am I free from struggle and pain.

THE LORD IN THE HEART: That is proof that you are lacking in surrender and patience. Why do you want to be free from trial and adversity? Why do you shun opposition? My peace is not of this world, but it is found when you are fully purified of all material desires, usually after many afflictions and having been thoroughly tried in the fire of tribulation.

If you think that you cannot bear it and that the suffering is too great, how will you endure the results of your sins in the future? Do you suppose that the torments of hell are easier to tolerate because they are in the future? If you cannot tolerate small things now for My sake, think of the unbearable agony you will suffer for the rebellious acts committed against Me. For the conditioned soul, there is always suffering, in both material and spiritual life, but an intelligent soul will choose the course that ends all pain. Therefore, to avoid future misery birth after birth, you should bear your present difficulties patiently for My sake, knowing that surrender brings ultimate relief and liberation.

THE SOUL: But why do I alone have to undergo so much purification and for so long?

THE LORD IN THE HEART: You are wrong again, My child. Do not think that others do not encounter torment in this world. Ask the sense enjoyers—the wine drinkers, gluttons, sexmongers, the greedy, rich, and powerful—call them all and ask them if they are free from anxiety and suffering. Even if you imagine that apart from some suffering, they are enjoying the intoxicating pleasures and opulences of this world, you should know that such pleasures last only for a season. But we are eternal. Think of it. All the pleasures of this world are but a flash, lasting for only a second—so brief, so false. How unintelligent to give them precedence over the pleasures of the spirit, which endure for all eternity! Only in drunken blindness and utter forgetfulness of Me would anyone trade his eternal birthright for a stinking pot of material sense enjoyment.

Give up your petty weakness of heart, My child, and turn away from the lusts of the flesh. Seek not your own desires, but seek My pleasure and My abode, where all your desires will be fulfilled. But you can never have both Me and another, or My kingdom and *maya's* simultaneously. Therefore abandon every attachment to this world. Hold in contempt every base delight and whatever else does not lead to Me. Strive always for the eternal, and shun what would distract you from it. Fix your attention on Me, and have no other shelter, for I am very much attracted to the helpless soul who has taken complete refuge in Me.

Do not expect complete success at once, for attachment to Me is awarded only to those whose hearts are wholly purified, and rarely without their having to endure great hardship, conflict, and struggle. Bad habits left over from many lifetimes of disobedience will rear up to defeat you, but they can be vanquished by new spiritual habits supported by the regulative principles of freedom. Great determination and enthusiasm can counteract even the anger of the material body when its senses are no longer indulged at their will. Although *maya* hurls every weapon she has in order to divert you from My service, be courageous and happy, for I am with you. Pray to Me, chant My Holy Name, and keep busy in My service. Do not doubt that I will protect you. It is My promise that My devotee will never perish.

☆☆☆☆☆☆☆☆☆☆☆☆☆☆

Meditation 51

Obedience Comes Before Chanting

THE SOUL: I try to pray often, my Lord, and I am always chanting Your Name and doing some useful service. What do I yet lack?

THE LORD IN THE HEART: Dear one, please listen to Me. It is not the mechanical following of a formula or the performance of set rituals that pleases Me. It is the loving surrender of the heart. Thus one who tries to avoid My smallest desire or disobeys My instructions cannot attain My mercy. Obedience is more than praying or chanting or anything else, for it indicates a gentle and submissive spirit. Nor should obedience be offered only to Me personally, but also to My devotees, especially the spiritual master. Indeed, no one can chant My Name offenselessly if he disobeys the orders of My representative. My pure devotee should be treated as My very Self. This is better than worshiping Me directly. Therefore, submit yourself enthusiastically to the spiritual master for advancement in Krishna consciousness, and thereby become master of the mind and senses.

The more quickly you learn to surrender to spiritual authority, the more quickly you will realize that you are not the material body but spirit soul, and thus attain Me. If you do not realize your spiritual nature through practical acts of devotion, how will you be able to conquer *maya*, the illusory energy that keeps you in bondage? Remember that if you have not learned to control the restless mind and senses, you are your own worst enemy. The subdued mind verily reflects Me, but the mind agitated by sense enjoyment carries the soul to hell. Therefore, with determination, subjugate the uncontrolled senses and mind, and in due course of time you will attain complete success.

It is due only to your perverted sense of self-love that you fear surrendering to Me or My servants. Even I Myself gladly agree to carry out the orders of My friends the Pandavas, or submit Myself to the chastisement of My father, Nanda Maharaj, and My Mother, Yasoda. Are you greater than I? Are you not but a spark of Me, an atom of My infinite Being? If I—the Supreme Personality of Godhead, the Lord of the universe, the Creator, Maintainer, and Destroyer of all that be—humbly submit Myself to My devotee, how much more should you become the servant of My servant? Only then will you be able to chant My Name and serve Me favorably.

Materially, you are but dust and clay, and spiritually you are infinitesimal, barely one ten-thousandth the size of the tip of a hair. Obey Me, obey My representatives, obey men when their orders are not contrary to My higher law. Learn to be humble, and break that stubborn will, which has separated you from Me for so many lifetimes. If you err, do so on the side of self-abnegation. Denigrate yourself. Let not one ounce of pride remain. Become lowly, like the blades of grass or the trees of the forest, which don't protest even if men trample them under foot or cut them down completely.

Who are you to complain, rebellious soul? How many times have you offended Me and My saints by your unwillingness to surrender? Usurping My property and imitating My position, you are the lowest of creatures, ungrateful even to the Master who feeds you. O vile demon, you are deserving of torment in hell and worse.

Yet I love you and come to reclaim you, for you are very precious to Me. Now listen to Me and know My love, that you may ever remain submissive to My will and never leave Me again.

☆☆☆☆☆☆☆☆☆☆☆☆☆☆☆

Meditation 52

Glory In God And Not In Yourself

THE SOUL: Sometimes You are as terrifying as a thunderbolt, my Lord, and sometimes You are as soft as a rose. Sometimes I weep in ecstasy, and sometimes I cry in fear. I want to love You with all my heart, but I am afraid. You see my every thought and deed, and that terrifies me. I know that in Your wrath You do not even spare Your sons: if they commit offenses, You duly punish them. On the other hand, You are so impartial that if even an enemy does something laudable, You reward him appropriately. Since I am most fallen and offensive, I am in anxiety thinking what You might do to me. I have seen some who were very advanced in Krishna consciousness fall down from Your service due to a small offense committed toward a devotee. Their whole devotional life has been ruined, just like a garden trampled by a mad elephant, and they have again returned to their former life of degradation, just like a dog returning to his vomit to eat it again. This is very frightening to me.

I have no hope but You, my Lord. If You do not uphold me with Your mighty arm and grasp me tight with Your mighty hand, I am sure to fall. Apart from Your association, there is no holiness; without Your guidance, there is no wisdom. If You fail to defend me, what is the use of courage? Without Your guardianship, I can be neither moral nor chaste. Vigilance is meaningless apart from Your watchfulness, for unless You see first, no one else can see. This whole world is full of darkness. Without Your light, I will remain in ignorance perpetually. My very nature is forgetfulness, and unless You have mercy on me and impart transcendental knowledge, I will sink further and further into the most degraded species of existence. Have mercy, O Lord, and save me, I pray. Left to myself, I am weak, but You can make me strong. My tendency is to grow cold, or at best, lukewarm, but You can fire me up and inspire me to perform things heretofore unimaginable.

Please, O my dear Friend Krishna, do not let me forget You. Let me remain lowly and humble in my own sight and disregard whatever appears to be of value in me. Whatever I have is Yours: it has come from You and is meant for Your service. Teach me Your ways and make me submissive to Your judgements.

Oh, how light and free I feel now! What an immeasurable weight I bore, thinking that I was lord and master, the doer, the enjoyer, and the sufferer! I am nothing, can be nothing, will be nothing but Your eternal servant. Nothing is mine, nothing can be mine, nothing will ever be mine. Nothing to protect, nothing to fear, nothing to gain. All is Yours, and I am Yours. Oh blessed repose, perfect peace! Falsity is vanquished, and pride has no place to hide. Vainglory is engulfed in devotional service to You, O Lord of the universe. Indeed, Your servants are so transcendentally satisfied that they would even reject changing places with You, if such were possible. Nor do they want any kind of liberation, like merging into Your impersonal existence. Those who aspire for material benedictions or mystic perfections are prone to pride and conceit. They engage in flattery and are affected by the flattery of others. But one who has placed all his hope in You is never deceived. This world will soon pass away, and all that is connected with it, including those attached to it. But You are eternal, I am eternal, and our love is eternal. This is the Supreme Absolute Truth that remains forever.

☆☆☆☆☆☆☆☆☆☆☆☆☆☆☆

Meditation 53

Speaking Silently

THE LORD IN THE HEART: One of the qualities of a devotee is silence. That stillness, however, is not the inability of the dumb or the deadness of stone. It is the absence of nonsensical material sounds, allowing you to hear My voice within and the voice of the spiritual master without. You should never speak what is useless and unnecessary simply for the pleasure of the flesh, nor should you speak words arising from mental speculation, the imperfect product of an uncontrolled mind, but you should speak about My glories and repeat My pastimes for the welfare of all creatures. You should also chant My Holy Name for the purification of your soul. In this way you will always speak what is truthful and beneficial for all.

Your speech should be simple and unaffected. Do not foolishly declare, "I have done such and such," and, "Tomorrow I will do such and such." But humbly say, "If it please You, my Lord, let it be so," or, "If You think it wise and good for me, O Lord, let me serve You thus." Or you should pray, "If, O God, my desire is not Your desire but is harmful to my spiritual well-being, please remove that desire and make my desires one with Yours."

Remember that not every desire comes from Me, even though you may think it very good. Indeed, it is sometimes difficult to discern between selfish desires and My desires, unless you are carefully guided by My word and by My representative. Many who professed to follow My path are now gone astray because they could not distinguish My desire from their own perverted longings for sense gratification. Therefore, test every desire presented by the mind to know its quality and be always guided by the scriptures and the bona fide spiritual master, for they never deviate from the Truth. Finally, place all things before Me with perfect surrender and pray without ceasing.

THE SOUL: Dear Lord Krishna, You are the all good Personality of Godhead, and You know everything, especially what is best for me. Do what You will, when You will, as much as You will, and surely I will be happy. You are the perfect Master and the only real Friend. I don't ask You for anything but to engage in Your service. Still, You give me more than I can ask. Your mercy and loving kindness are inexhaustible. Have mercy on me, for I am most fallen, and no one else can help me. Place me as one of the atoms at Your Lotus Feet, and deal with me according to Your loving pleasure. You are the potter, and I am the clay. I am helpless in Your hands; You can turn me whatever way You wish, for You are the Supreme Artist who turns spirit into matter and matter into spirit.

Grant me strength, O God, that I may serve You to the very end. Let my will become one with Yours, that we may be united in loving desire. Let me will nothing contrary to Your desire, but give me the will to satisfy Your every desire. Grant me the determination to die to all pleasures not meant for Your pleasure alone, and to live for Your honor only and not my own. Grant me the peace that comes to a devotee who gives up his life in perfect Krishna consciousness, fully engaged in Your service. In this world there is no peace, but in You there is perfect peace, for You, Lord Narayan, are the resting place of all living entities.

☆☆☆☆☆☆☆☆☆☆☆☆☆☆☆☆

Meditation 54

You Are My Only Refuge, O Lord

THE SOUL: Everyone knows that there is no safety in a sinking ship, yet, O God, I often forget that this material body is going down day by day and minute by minute and that soon I will have to leave it behind. What happiness can there be in anything so transitory? Indeed, this body is always causing me great anxiety and pain. Why am I so insanely attached to it? If I really want peace and happiness, I have to look beyond this mortal dream to something substantial and real. Even if I gain the whole world, what is its value? How long can it endure? Family, friends, society, or whatever—what can they really do for me? Will they be there when death comes? Will they be able to help me cross over that great ocean separating the living from the dead? O my God, help me, for You will be my only shelter in that hour of need. You are the only one who still cares for me when all others are gone. Therefore I take refuge in You alone.

Now let me put aside the inane pursuit of pleasure and the foolish squandering of the opportunity afforded by human life. This is my chance for self-realization. Material life, with all its opportunities for sense gratification, is available in every form of life, but a human being can understand and love You, the very Source of life. The more I try to enjoy my present external situation, so briefly manifested, the greater the chance I will miss my eternally blissful life with You. Teach me to value every moment and use material things in Your service only. In this way I will not fall under the control of the modes of nature, which force me to accept sinful and pious reactions and thus repeated birth and death. Make me satisfied with whatever you allot and free me from attachment and aversion.

You are all merciful, O Lord. By Your grace and in accordance with past activities, the living entity enters a particular mother's womb, where Your material nature gives him a suitable body to fulfill his desires. Out of 8,400,000 different species of life, one rarely attains to human life with its highly developed consciousness meant for understanding You. This consciousness is not available to the dogs and hogs, nor, in general, to the residents of heavenly planets. As far as sense pleasures are concerned, everyone in every species enjoys them in due course of time, even without trying, just as in time we experience suffering without seeking it. Who can understand the workings of Your *maya?*

Be merciful to me, dear Lord, and release me from the bondage of illusion. I am Your eternal fragment, but somehow or other I have fallen into this ocean of misery. Save me from thinking myself anything other than Your eternal servant. Grant that I may never forget You and that I may always chant Your Holy Name. How glorious is that Holy Name! Even if one is born in a family of dog-eaters, he becomes worshipable by chanting Your Name. It is not necessary to perform great sacrifices, study Vedic knowledge, or undergo severe penance and austerities; one is elevated to the highest transcendental position as soon as he chants Your Holy Name.

No one can fathom Your mercy by which You have made Yourself easily available in the sound of Your Name. But I am such a failure that I cannot even take Your mercy. You are anxiously waiting to dance on my tongue, but I am such a miser that I cannot appreciate Your gift. Take pity on me, O Krishna, and promise me that sometime—if not in this life then in some other—I shall be able to chant Your Holy Names just once with sincere feeling: Hare Krishna, Hare Krishna, Krishna Krishna, Hare Hare, Hare Rama, Hare Rama, Rama Rama, Hare Hare.

☆☆☆☆☆☆☆☆☆☆☆☆☆☆☆

Meditation 55

Have Faith In Me Alone

THE LORD IN THE HEART: My dear friend, you should allow Me to do whatever I desire, for I am your ever Well-wisher, and know what is truly good for you. Being a conditioned soul, you are apt to commit mistakes. You also have imperfect senses and are subject to illusion, and besides, you have a cheating propensity. Trust only in Me, and I will deliver you from every imperfection.

THE SOUL: I know that whatever You say is true, my Lord. You are the greatest Friend, and You care for me even better than I can care for myself. How foolish I am when I mistrust Your motives and think You to be like an ordinary human being, thus committing offenses at Your Lotus Feet! You want only to save me from this rotten material existence and take me back home, back to Godhead, but due to my envious nature, I think that You are trying to take something away from me and that You don't want me to enjoy as I see You enjoy. Thinking that I am separate from You, I imagine myself to be Your competitor. But You, my Lord, have no competitor, for You are the One without a second, the Lord and Master of all. Kindly overlook my offenses, just as a mother overlooks the offenses of her unborn child kicking in her womb. You are an ocean of mercy, and You are compassion personified. Look kindly upon Your servant and do with me whatever pleases You, for whatever You do is good beyond all measure.

Being now imprisoned by imperfect senses, I think that health and wealth are to be desired, but with Your perfect vision You afflict my body and take away all my possessions. Let me praise Your unlimited mercy.

Because I identify myself with my fickle mind, I think that knowledge is to be sought and ignorance to be shunned; but You, my Lord, confound the learned and reveal Yourself to the simple. Let me proclaim Your glories from the rooftops. Even when You make me brokenhearted, hiding Your transcendental face from me, I will chant Your Holy Name unceasingly, for there is no difference between You and Your Name.

THE LORD IN THE HEART: My dear little friend, I very much appreciate your submissive attitude. This is the only qualification for always abiding in My love. If you wish to walk with Me, you must be ready to accept any material condition—suffering or enjoyment, opulence or destitution. Make Me your treasure, and be satisfied in Me alone. Thus you will live happily with Me forever.

But those who neglect My instructions and rebel against My authority can never be happy, either in this life or the next. They must again descend to the lower species to reap the results of their sinful activities.

My dear friend, do not belittle My word, for it is for your benefit. One who has been awarded this human form of life should not work hard day and night simply for sense gratification, which is available even for the stool-eating dogs and hogs. You should always engage in penance and austerity to attain the divine life of devotional service. By such activity, one's heart is purified, and thus purified, one attains eternal, blissful life, transcendental to material happiness. Even if you sometimes fall down due to immaturity, there is no danger of ultimately failing. On the other hand, there is no chance of success for a materialist or a non-devotee, even if he gains the whole world, for his soul is lost.

THE SOUL: O my dear Lord Krishna, I totally accept whatever You say. I shall gladly endure whatever You desire. From Your hand I can accept good and bad equally, for You are all good. From Your mouth I will take the bitter and the sweet; whatever proceeds from You is pure nectar. Happiness and distress, joy and sorrow have lost all meaning, since existence with You is uncontaminated bliss, beyond all duality. Therefore, let me always be grateful for whatever comes from Your hand, my Lord. I pray only that You keep me from sin and disobedience. If You do, then even death and hell cannot frighten me. If only I could remember You and chant Your Holy Name, I would prefer hell itself to all the pleasures of heaven enjoyed in forgetfulness of You. I fall at Your Lotus Feet again and again. O Krishna, do not kick me away. I am Your servant eternally. Have mercy upon me. Have mercy upon me.

☆☆☆☆☆☆☆☆☆☆☆☆☆☆

Meditation 56

Others Have Endured More Than You

THE LORD IN THE HEART: My friend, although I am the Fountainhead of existence, I live in the heart of every spirit soul, directing his wanderings and fulfilling all desires. No one forces Me to descend thus to this mortal world, but out of love for you, My part and parcel, I come again and again, not only as Supersoul, the Lord in the heart, but in My various incarnations as well. Whenever there is a decline in real religion or proper execution of duty, I descend, either personally or through My empowered representative. In this way, the path of real religion—surrender to Me—is reestablished. Those opposed to Me are annihilated. My devotees are thus made happy by witnessing My transcendental pastimes. But do not imagine that this is accomplished without hardship and difficulty for My devotees. Their greatness, however, is in never losing faith in Me and in tolerating all kinds of adversities. In the end, My divine plan is accomplished, for no one can thwart My will. Furthermore, it is My promise that My devotee will never perish.

Consider My devotee Prahlad. He was a lad of only five years, and committed no offense other than being My devotee. But for this, his demoniac father became extremely angry and tried to kill him in many ways: by poisoning him, boiling him in oil, throwing him into a pit of snakes and off a mountain cliff. Still, Prahlad, remaining steady in his faith in Me, was unafraid. Thus, I delivered him in My wonderful form of Lord Nrisingha.

Consider also My pure devotee Haridas Thakur. Simply because he always chanted My Holy Name, he was whipped through twenty-two marketplaces. Finally his torturers dropped from exhaustion, while he continued to chant my Holy Names. Previously, no one had ever lived through more than two or three such lashings, but he survived twenty-two. How is this possible? Because I have promised to protect the soul surrendered to Me, I personally accepted the lacerations on My own body to save My devotee. Have faith, My friend. What has been endured by others can also be borne by you, if you but trust in Me and accept My protection. From the lives of these great souls, learn to depend on Me alone.

THE SOUL: My Lord, You are an ocean of mercy, and Your devotees are the personification of all good qualities. Out of their great love for You, they can easily tolerate all the disturbances offered by the material energy. Please allow me, a most fallen sinner, to follow in their footsteps by waiting upon Your desires eternally. Grant me the patience to endure the miseries of material life, knowing that they are ultimately for the purification of the soul. Give me the realization that even my mistakes and failures can become transcendental benedictions. After all, You are the most expert Mystic who can make everything culminate in a blessing for those who surrender to Your Lotus Feet. Why do men fear surrendering to You, the very Soul of their soul? Why do they fear what is good and beneficial for them? What will they lose, but their illusion and bondage?

O my dearest Friend, Krishna, I can never adequately thank You for showing me the way out of this darkness of ignorance, back to the light of the Spiritual Sky, Your eternal abode. You are so kind that even when I was far away, You did not forget me. When I neglected You in every way possible, You were still attentive to my welfare. You are so loving that when I was most fallen, You sent Your most confidential friend, the bona fide spiritual master, to proclaim Your message loud and clear and thus rouse my sleeping soul to Krishna consciousness. Had You not come, had he not come, how could we know and follow Your steps? Divine grace flows from the Fountain of grace. Thank you, Lord Krishna. Thank you, Srila Prabhupada.

☆☆☆☆☆☆☆☆☆☆☆☆☆☆

130

Meditation 57

Surrender To Suffering

THE LORD IN THE HEART: Yes, you thank Me now, when you have good health and plenty of sense gratification, but what will you say when I take it all away? Will you not complain when there is no result for your endeavor, no success for your works, no credit or praise for your hard labor? What if you receive only blame, defamation, abuse, persecution, or even death for engaging in My service? What will you say then, My child? Thus far you have met very little resistance, but many have been cursed and beaten and even killed for My sake. Yet they were faithful to the end, and they overcame every temptation. Remember the tribulations of these great souls, and you will bear your own small ones quite easily. When you think that they are not small but too great to bear, test your endurance and try your patience. Then your surrender to Me will increase. As you surrender to Me, I reward you accordingly, just as whatever face you present to the mirror is the one you see. In any case, I Myself delight in becoming the servant of My servant, for this is the relationship of love.

The more you become submissive in tribulation, the easier it is to realize My plan for you and therefore My divine mercy. Train your mind and senses to accept sufferings gladly for My sake. Do not hesitate or complain, and do not say, "I cannot accept this situation, or tolerate this person. They're not fair to me, but I will surrender over here to this situation for as long as I think it is good for me."

Such thoughts denote either gross foolishness or an outright cheating mentality. They show a lack of appreciation for the virtue of true surrender, and the One to whom surrender is offered. Moreover, they falsely place the feelings and judgements of the conditioned soul in a superior position, and this prolongs his illusion. Even ordinary worldly persons tolerate what they like from whom they like. How would you be any different? My devotee who has surrendered everything to Me does not consider whether those from whom My tests come are superior, inferior, or equal, whether they are holy and good or evil and perverse. No matter how great the adversity, or how often it comes, My devotee receives it with gratitude. Indeed, in all things he sees My hand and accepts everything as coming from Me. Thus in all conditions he is happy by My grace.

But such realization is not to be had without struggle and contention. Without great effort, the crest jewel of surrender cannot be won, and failure to try is to lose by default. Everything is situated on desire. If you but prove your desire by honest endeavor, I will surely help you. Have faith, my little one. Your enemies are already slain by My arrangement, and you can be but My instrument in the battle. Therefore, My friend, get up and fight. Victory is yours if you fight manfully and depend on My mercy. Fight the good fight. Without fighting there is no victory, just as without hard labor there is no rest.

THE SOUL: What You say, my Lord, seems quite impossible. You know that I am very weak and have but little faith, and that I am easily discouraged by the slightest reverse. Help me, O God. On Your order, I want to act, but You must help me.

Now let the miseries of material life hurl their arrows at me with all their might. Let calamities come and wreak their worst. Let me suffer unlimitedly for all the offenses I have committed at Your Lotus Feet. It does not matter. My existence of separate desire is now over, and You are at my side, guiding me, steadying me, empowering me to act on Your behalf. If You are for me, who can be against me? O Krishna, I take shelter of You now and forevermore.

☆☆☆☆☆☆☆☆☆☆☆☆☆

Meditation 58

Material Life Means Weakness And Misery

THE SOUL: Without You, my Lord, I am weak and helpless. The waves of material life threaten to engulf me, and there is no place to hide.

Frequently, when a slight thing upsets and discourages me, I doubt You and become morose and cannot execute my duty. Often I vow to act religiously, but I falter at the least difficulty. Sometimes I become terribly agitated by the most trifling thing, or sometimes, when I am feeling very strong and safe, *maya* suddenly strikes without notice, and I am overcome. Although I am confessing this to You, my Lord, You already know my fallen condition and frailty of heart. But since You are known as the Savior of the most fallen, my claim is first. Have mercy upon this wretched soul, and lift me out of the filth of material existence. Without Your help, I am without hope and forever despondent.

Prone to slip under the control of my passions, I feel oppressed and want to flee from Your sight. Even when I do not actually yield to these passions, their constant assault wearies me, and I despair. How long will this daily strife afflict me? Why do sinful fantasies come more easily than they go? When will I see the day of my freedom from this stinking flesh? My helplessness is suffocating me.

It is now in Your hands, O Krishna. You can make me or break me. That power is Yours. But as the Lover of surrendered souls, please have compassion on me, the lowest of Your servants, and assist me in all my endeavors on Your behalf. Infuse me with transcendental life to realize my higher nature, lest I continue to identify myself with this dead body and thus be forced to accept body after body in an unending repetition of birth and death.

Alas! What more can be said of this life, which is nothing but one misery after another? From the moment of birth, we are crying; as we grow, we endure sickness and disease; in old age, we suffer infirmity and remorse; and finally death destroys all hope. It is a life fraught with snares and enemies. Before one encounter is ended, another begins. Indeed, often many others attack unexpectedly, even before the first attacker desists. How can one love a life so devoid of meaning and so filled with bitterness, calamity, and misery? Is it not strange that we call life what is more aptly characterized as suffering and death? From the time of birth our life is being wrenched from us, moment by moment, day by day, until there is no more left. *Maya's* greatest trick must be in deluding us into thinking that we can enjoy this mortal life. Thus she beguiles us into giving up our life of eternity, knowledge, and bliss with You for the ruse of sense pleasure, which always ends in misery.

I have heard many wise men declare this world to be false, yet they can hardly give it up due to their strong attachment to the pleasures of the flesh. Everyone knows that this is a world of duality—heat and cold, happiness and distress, pleasure and pain—and that some things cause us to love the world and some to despise it. The pleasurable objects of the senses, the attachments of the mind, and the influence of the illusory energy cause us to love it; and the miseries of material life—birth, death, old age, and disease—which are the natural results of those sense objects, bring detachment and hatred for this world. Therefore, it is better that calamities and misfortunes befall me again and again so that I may loathe this material world and in my suffering think of You constantly, and thus not have to undergo repetition of birth and death.

O sinful illusion that beguiles us all, using vicious pleasure to cover the soul in forgetfulness of You! Like the camel, who chews thorns and relishes the taste of his own blood and saliva, we think that there are hidden pleasures beneath the thorns of sense gratification. But we are sucking our own blood, calling death very near and naming it enjoyment. Oh fool that I am! Who can deliver me? Who will show me that real sweetness, love of God, by which one loses all attachment to temporal things and lives in an ocean of bliss? Your devotees know this ecstasy of eternal love and freely give it to all who sincerely seek Your protection. Therefore, let me take shelter of them, and bow down to them continually. Let me serve them always, without duplicity, for they are very dear to You, Lord Krishna, and You are very dear to them.

☆☆☆☆☆☆☆☆☆☆☆☆☆

Meditation 59

You Are The Greatest, My Lord

THE LORD IN THE HEART: Yes, you are right, My child. You must take shelter of My pure devotees and inquire from them very sincerely about Me, for they are very compassionate of heart and anxious to help all who diligently seek Me. Learn from them through practical service, but beware of envy. Envy of My devotee is sure death to spiritual life. Become a menial slave for My sake, and you will soon find Me.

THE SOUL: O Krishna, Lord of my heart, You are so kind to me. Not only do You reside with me in all conditions, but You send your bona fide representative, the spiritual master, to personally guide me back home, back to Godhead. How great a Friend You are! Despite my pigheaded plans for material happiness, you expertly arrange everything to frustrate my designs. Lovingly You prod me to take up the progressive path of devotional service to Your Lordship. Who can imagine the bliss, happiness, peace, and eternal rest that are to be found upon giving up everything and taking shelter of You alone? Truly, my Lord, You are above all and within all, and You are the end of all. Everything rests in You. In You alone can I find lasting peace.

Grant me, O Govinda, the vision of Your three-curved bending form. You stand playing on Your flute and inviting Your devotees to sing and dance in the ecstasy of eternal love. Such thoughts immediately transport my mind far, far beyond this material sky, above every creature, above all considerations of health or fame or wealth or power or honor or praise or knowledge or accomplishment, even above joy and happiness, sweetness and ecstasy, merit and reward, above any pleasure in this world or in heaven. I want You, my Lord—nothing more and nothing less.

Intellectual fools speculate about You, but their grammatical skill and word jugglery cannot attract You nor save them at the moment of death. If they would just worship You with a pure heart and follow in the footsteps of Your pure devotees, they would understand You very easily. You are the Origin of all. Your form is eternity, knowledge, and bliss. You are the Cause of all causes. Although Your body is not like that of an ordinary living entity, fools and rascals think that You are one of us because You condescend to live among us. They do not know Your higher nature, supreme and unchangeable. There is no difference between Your body and soul, for You are Absolute. Any one of Your transcendental senses can perform the actions of any or all of Your other senses. No one can be greater than You or even equal to You, my Lord. You are inconceivable to our tiny brains. But on the other hand, You reveal Yourself as You are to Your surrendered soul—full knowledge, unending existence, and entire bliss.

O Govinda, let me fall down at Your Lotus Feet and worship You again and again. You are the primeval Lord, the Father of all. You are eternally engaged in tending spiritual cows that fulfill all desires, and You live in celestial palaces built of spiritual gems. Your gardens are surrounded by millions of desire trees, and You are served continually with great reverence and affection by hundreds and thousands of Goddesses of Fortune. Who can be equal to You?

O Govinda, primal God, dearmost Friend! Your flute playing cannot be rivaled in the three worlds. Your eyes are as enchanting as the newly blown lotus, and Your head is decorated with a peacock's feather. Your beautiful dark body is tinged with the hue of a summer rain cloud. Indeed, Your unique loveliness charms and defeats even Cupid. Who can resist Your call?

O Govinda, where have You gone? Why are You hiding from me? Of what use are eyes that cannot see You? Is there not someone who can save me from this hell of not seeing You constantly? That, only You can do, my Lord. You are the Controller of everyone, and everything is within Your power. I am begging You, come back. I promise You whatever You want. Do anything to me, take anything from me, but please be merciful to me. Kindly smear my eyes with the ointment of eternal love so that I can see Your transcendental form constantly and thus relieve the burning of my heart. No other benediction, no other salvation or liberation, nothing—only You, dear Shyamasundara, only You.

☆☆☆☆☆☆☆☆☆☆☆☆☆☆☆☆

Meditation 60

Your Mercy Is Immeasurable, O God

THE LORD IN THE HEART: I am always with you, My dear child, but you do not always realize My presence. Sometimes I may appear before you, and then again I may withdraw Myself. This is also My mercy, meant to increase your hankering for Me. I can be seen constantly only by those who, free from all material contamination, do not desire anything within the three worlds other than Me. Be peaceful, My little one. You are resting safely in the hollow of My hand, and I will never let you go nor let any harm befall you. You are My chosen vessel, and I have much to accomplish through you.

THE SOUL: I bow to You, O Lord, for You are the very Source of my life. Without You, there is no meaning to anything. Indeed, without You, there is nothing at all. We cannot see unless You see first, nor hear unless You hear first, nor think nor move nor feel. You are the Source of all consciousness and the Master of the senses. Help me, O Hrisikesa, for I want to surrender to You completely.

Open my mind and heart to Your instruction and lead me in the paths of righteousness. Give me the knowledge and wisdom to understand Your ways and the strength and courage to execute Your orders in every circumstance. Give me remembrance and not forgetfulness so that I may eagerly engage in Your service, fully conscious of the privilege and responsibility of being Your servant. Your loving kindness is unlimitedly showered upon me. Let me meditate upon Your causeless mercy that comes to me every second of my life. I thank You again and again.

Sometimes *maya* comes and tempts me, saying, "Another has received more mercy than you." But everything is Yours, my Lord, and You are free to do whatever pleases You. If you give more to one and less to another, You know, through Your infinite wisdom, that it is best. You are best, and whatever You do is also best. According to our past activities, we are wandering throughout the universe in different species. Sometimes we are elevated to the heavenly planets, and sometimes, due to disobedience to Your law, degraded to hellish life. You are equally kind to everyone, for You are simply fulfilling our desires as expressed by our activities. When someone gets a chance, by Your causeless mercy, to associate with Your pure devotee, he is awarded the greatest boon: the seed of devotion to Your Lordship.

Thus, we should never be proud, thinking that we have received more blessing than another. It is only through Your mercy and not our good deeds that success or failure comes. As soon as I attribute anything good to myself, I become bad, for I am attempting to usurp Your position as the all good. Therefore, let me ascribe less to myself; help me become more humble and devout in giving all thanks to You. Being lower than all others, I am least worthy of Your blessings. However, it is precisely when I realize my own inadequacies that You bestow a double share of Your blessings. No one can fathom Your divine grace and infinite mercy.

Now let the glory be Yours, for just as a light-colored subject appears more brilliant against a dark background, so You show mercy to the most fallen, and You appear more glorious for it. In the form of Lord Chaitanya, You have shown the greatest mercy, teaching us real knowledge, devotional service, and detachment from all that does not foster Krishna consciousness. Lord Chaitanya is an ocean of mercy, freely giving what was formerly very difficult to attain—pure love of Krishna.

He is personally demonstrating the *yuga-dharma*, the path of salvation for this age, by leading the *sankirtana* movement, chanting Your Holy Names: Hare Krishna, Hare Krishna, Krishna Krishna, Hare Hare; Hare Rama, Hare Rama, Rama Rama, Hare Hare. Let me surrender unto His Lotus Feet.

☆☆☆☆☆☆☆☆☆☆☆☆☆☆

Meditation 61

The Eightfold Path To Peace

THE LORD IN THE HEART: Now, my little one, listen carefully as I tell you of the eightfold path to peace, which brings to an end all material miseries:

—Know that I am the Ultimate Goal of all existence: after many, many births of culturing knowledge, one comes to know that I am all that exists.

—Recognize that I am the actual Proprietor, the rightful owner of everything. Those who do not recognize this fall down into hellish life.

—Admit that I am the only real Enjoyer. When others are enjoyed by Me, they also feel satisfied.

—Understand all these, and you will realize that I am the best Friend of all living beings.

These four truths about My supreme nature lead to perfect peace.

Now hear of their practical application:

—Become the servant of My servant and learn to prefer others to yourself by rendering menial service to them and placing yourself beneath all men.

—Know the wealth of poverty, and for yourself choose less rather than more.

—Do unto others as you would have them do unto you, and you will perceive My presence in all.

—Pray unceasingly to be fully surrendered to My will. Those who diligently follow this path of Mine attain lasting peace and rest in Me.

THE SOUL: My dear Lord, Your words are brief but exceedingly profound. If only I could perfectly execute these instructions, I would enjoy great spiritual benefit. Certainly I would not be so easily disturbed, nor would I become discouraged in my service or morose over the results. It is only because I have failed to heed Your advice that I am so slow to advance in Krishna consciousness. Still, You are very patient with me and always anxious for my well-being. Therefore, I pray to You, who can do anything and everything, to increase my faith and determination to follow Your path without deviation.

Grant me, O God, protection from the uncontrolled mind, which comes as a thief to take away my concentration on Your Lotus Feet. Sometimes unwanted thoughts and great fears overwhelm me. Will You not protect me and save my soul from endless transmigration?

Light up my heart, O Krishna, with the torchlight of knowledge. Remove the long shadows of *maya* and the darkness of forgetfulness. Call back my wandering thoughts and render the temptations of the flesh null and void by Your all-attractive presence. Help me, my Lord, for these evil foes attack me most violently, and unless You protect me, I will surely perish.

☆☆☆☆☆☆☆☆☆☆☆☆☆☆☆

141

Meditation 62

Save Yourself First

THE LORD IN THE HEART: Why are you so busy worrying about others, to the neglect of your own destiny? To distribute My love to others and enlighten them about their eternal nature is good, but idle curiosity about the business of others must be avoided. What does it matter what they are doing? If you do right, that is the greatest good you can do, and that example will help others also. Don't concern yourself with what another is doing, saying, or thinking. You will never be called upon to answer for him, but you will be accountable for yourself, even for the slightest deviation. Therefore, do not waste time meddling in the affairs of others, but be diligent in your duty, knowing that this is the path of perfection.

You should know that as the Lord in the heart of all creatures, I know all that has happened in the past and all that is to come. I know all men, what they think and what they do, but Me, no one knows. That is the difference between you and Me: you are but a part of Me, an infinitesimal fragment of My eternal being, one with Me in quality, but vastly smaller in quantity. Thus, while I am eternally cognizant of all, you have a tendency to forget and come under the influence of My illusory nature. Therefore, you should surrender to Me, and commit all things to My divine care, that you may remain always at peace. What will all your worry accomplish? Can you, by all your wishing, make one hair black or one hair white? With all your effort, can you make the sun shine or the rain fall? Just try to understand that all things happen by My will, according to My desire and not according to yours. Man proposes God disposes. My ways are far above your ways, and My thoughts above yours. I am perfect in everything I do. Just surrender to Me, and all your worries will be over, for I will give you all that you need.

Have faith in Me, My child, and be peaceful under My protection. Let others be disturbed and restless as they will. Indeed, I fulfill the desires of everyone, but those who surrender to Me receive one gift and those who resist Me receive another. I am as impartial as a wish-fulfilling tree, but to you, My friend, I give perfect knowledge. Do not be illusioned by My external nature. Do not seek the shadow of name and fame, or the praise of men. Such things only distract you from My service and bring darkness of vision and heaviness of heart. Listen to Me carefully, for I want to reveal My innermost secret to you. This is not revealed to mental speculators, nor to fruitive workers, nor even to mystic yogis, but only to My pure devotee. Therefore just try sincerely to approach My pure devotee, and inquire from him submissively about the Absolute Truth. Be ready to render any service to him, just as you would to Me, for he is My representative. Because he is very kind— more kind than I—he will engage You in My service and teach you all things. Then you will know the perfect Truth of My eternal love.

Be humble, be watchful, be prudent. Accept My special mercy by always chanting My Name. Never doubt that he who perseveres to the end will find life's ultimate goal—pure love of God.

☆☆☆☆☆☆☆☆☆☆☆☆☆☆

Meditation 63

Peace And Progress Are In Me

THE LORD IN THE HEART: My dear child, I certainly want to see you happy and enjoying all good fortune in this world and the next. You also desire these things but do not know how they are attained. The devoted soul who offers the results of all his activities to Me attains unadulterated peace and happiness, whereas a person whose desires are not one with Mine, who is greedy to enjoy the fruits of his labor, becomes entangled in the reactions of work and thus undergoes repeated birth and death.

If you actually desire real peace, you must carefully cultivate those qualities that bring it about. Peace certainly comes to the knower of Truth, but it is the result of self-control, austerity, purity, tolerance, honesty, wisdom, knowledge, and religiousness. Develop these qualities, and peace will follow, just as a dutiful wife follows her husband.

THE SOUL: This seems very difficult, my Lord. How can I do it?

THE LORD IN THE HEART: Be careful in what you say and what you do. To prevent an indiscretion is always easier than to correct one. Yet, it is not from your striving that these qualities manifest. Verily, they appear spontaneously, without extra endeavor, in the bodies of My pure devotees. Therefore, become My devotee by always thinking of

Me. Mold your every desire upon Mine and work diligently for My satisfaction. Concentrate on self-improvement by means of self-sacrifice and self-effacement. Meditate on your own faults, not on the faults of others. When you practice seeing the good in others, the good in you will grow by leaps and bounds. In this way, avoiding disturbance to yourself and others, you will enjoy an atmosphere of transcendental bliss.

This does not mean that difficulties and suffering will never come your way. Material life means suffering, even for My devotees. Even My mother, Devaki, suffered the loss of all her children, and My friends the Pandavas lost their kingdom. Uninterrupted bliss is to be found only in My eternal abode. Do not confuse times of elation, freedom from depression, and material comfort with spiritual blessedness, nor think that everything is perfect just because it suits your sensibilities. Nor should you think that you are more beloved by Me because at the moment you are displaying great devotion and dedication. A man of real virtue is more than circumstance, and so is the path of progress and perfection.

THE SOUL: What more can there be, My Lord?

THE LORD IN THE HEART: More than this and more than all else, surrender to My divine will, not out of force or fear or hope for some material benediction, but simply out of love. If you do not think yourself separate from Me in little matters of daily routine, your desires will be one with Me in great and eternal matters. If you are always equipoised and indifferent to happiness and distress, knowing all things to be My mercy, you will properly see Me everywhere.

You should become so filled with faith and love for Me that you determine in your heart to suffer even death for My sake, not caring for praise or adoration. In tribulation, you should not try to vindicate yourself as if you did not deserve to suffer so much, but should feel yourself the most fallen, lower than the lowest, and deserving of much greater punishment for all your past offenses against Me. Thus acknowledging My justice, goodness, and infinite mercy, you will be able to chant My Holy Name with feeling. Then you will know the eternal path of peace.

I am hidden from the proud and haughty, but I am seen face to face by the pure in heart. Have faith, my child, have faith. I am with you always.

☆☆☆☆☆☆☆☆☆☆☆☆☆☆☆☆

Meditation 64

Free Indeed

THE SOUL: It is often said, O Lord, that the mind is a thing in itself and can make a heaven of hell or a hell of heaven. The mind placed under Your control, Lord, is the hallmark of a perfect man, but the uncontrolled mind, turning on itself, is self-destructive. Be the ruler of my mind, O Krishna, and subdue my passions. Let me never relax my concentration on the things of the spirit, which are eternal and pleasing to You. Then I may safely pass through life undisturbed by the sirens' song of sense delight or the Sisyphean cares of material existence. Keep me free from indolence, and grant me, I pray, a mind unattached to the mundane and temporal.

Dear Lord Krishna, I am so weak and prone to distraction. I beg You to help me remain fixed at Your Lotus Feet, free from the cares of this world. *Maya's* allurements are so strong that if You do not protect me, I will surely be entangled. Show me the beauty of plain living and high thinking, lest I be attracted by the flickering beauty of flesh. Enlighten my mind with divine knowledge, lest it be filled with the darkness of material desire and I stumble into the pit of forgetfulness of You. I do not ask relief from the miseries of phenomenal existence, which fools try to counteract by ever greater doses of intoxicating sense pleasure, but I pray for deliverance from the unbearable misery of separation from You. Unless You mitigate my isolation and loneliness, how can I be truly free?

O Govinda, form of incomparable beauty, make all carnal comforts repulsive and make bitter the temporary pleasures that divert me from Your service to that of Your base reflections. Protect me, my Lord, and reveal Your real form to me moment by moment. Deliver me from the illusion that I am this body and that sense pleasure is happiness. Let neither worldly charm rob me of the boon of human life nor the wiles of the tempter trick me into trading my eternal Krishna consciousness for the sop of material gratification. Save me, O God. Grant this tiny speck of Your energy the courage and strength to resist temptation, the intelligence and patience to endure tribulation, and the wisdom and steady determination to be fixed eternally in Your loving service. Let the love of Your Holy Name be my only love and the chanting of Your Name my only consolation. You have so kindly made Yourself easily available in the sound of Your Name. Why do I not chant that divine sound constantly?

Without Your presence, I do not care to live. Even the necessities of life such as eating and sleeping are burdensome without You. Give me the spiritual intelligence to use all gifts for Your service: to eat or sleep no more than necessary, to accept everything favorable for Your service, and to reject everything unfavorable. To neglect things that can be used for Your pleasure is another snare of *maya*. You have created all things good. If we but use them properly, there can be no contamination. Still, being very deceptive, the mind can make us think that the trivial is important, and the important trivial. Without Your guidance, my Lord, I will surely err. Enlighten my mind and purify my heart that my spirit may be eternally free in Your love. If You make me free, My Lord, then shall I be free indeed.

☆☆☆☆☆☆☆☆☆☆☆☆☆☆

Meditation 65

Love Only Me

THE LORD IN THE HEART: I advise you, My dear child, to trust in Me alone and place all your confidence in Me. Have no faith in yourself, and do not depend on your own understanding. Self-love is the greatest delusion and the greatest cause of bondage. To whatever degree you identify with the senses, you will hanker and lament according to their dictation. But if your love is true, simple, and pure, you will remain free and never be a slave to anyone or anything. Therefore, do not covet what I have not given you, nor try to possess My gifts longer than I have ordained. Just surrender to Me, and I will make you really free.

Why do you not yield to Me completely, with all your heart? Why do you desire to possess anything apart from Me? After all, I am the Source of everything. Why do you destroy yourself with foolish sorrow and unnecessary worry? Is not your life of constant endeavor for ephemeral objects tiresome and frustrating? Submit yourself to My will, and I will preserve what you have and supply what you lack.

If you long for what you do not have, or to be where you are not, or to enjoy more comfort and ease than I have given, you will lack the freedom from anxiety and lasting peace that are the soul's natural condition. It is a vain imagination to think that somewhere in this world everything is enjoyable and everyone likeable. Misery and distress are common factors in all material situations. The striving for economic advancement and the aggrandizement of material things will never help you, but renouncing them, or better yet, using them only for My satisfaction brings complete relief. This applies not only to pleasure in the form of the gross objects but also to its subtle forms such as profit, adoration, and distinction. Shun material rewards and the praise of men. This world and everything in it will soon pass away. To seers of Truth, the world is no more than an empty dream.

You may change your location, but if your consciousness remains the same, what will change? If you dress a dog in a new suit and place him on a golden throne, does he become a king? Throw him an old shoe or a bloody bone, and his real character will immediately manifest. Peace and happiness are to be found not externally but in the heart that is at peace with Me and satisfied with Me alone. Beware of the false promises of *maya*, lest you be cheated of your present advantages and your latter state be worse than your former.

THE SOUL: Protect me by Your grace, O Krishna, and strengthen me in my determination to render devotional service, regardless of circumstances. Cleanse my heart of all mean motives and fix my hopes on perfection alone. Remove every attachment that is not rooted in You, and grant me the realization that You are all in all. Help me to regard everything material as a dream, temporary and insubstantial, and to discern that without connection to Your service, everything is vain and troublesome to the spirit. Distinguishing between the temporal and the eternal brings great wisdom and true intelligence.

Lord of the universe and Lord of my heart, impart understanding to my soul so that I may seek You above all else and find enjoyment and love in Your service and that of Your servants. Grant me the perfect vision to see You in every atom and perceive Your perfect will directing the wanderings of every living being. Perfect my hearing that I may hear the trees and creepers, the birds and beasts, the demons and devotees, and all other creatures great and small praising Your infinite greatness and chanting Your Holy Name. Then I shall also sing and dance in ecstasy, chanting, Hare Krishna, Hare Krishna, Krishna Krishna, Hare Hare, Hare Rama, Hare Rama, Rama Rama, Hare Hare.

☆☆☆☆☆☆☆☆☆☆☆☆☆☆

Meditation 66

The Lord Is Our Only Hope

THE LORD IN THE HEART: When men misjudge you and speak vilely about you for My sake, be happy, My child. Great, indeed, is your reward in My Kingdom. Do not feel the slightest resentment. Rather, bless them and try to instruct them in Krishna consciousness for their eternal well-being. You should feel grateful that they do not do worse to you, as you know that you have done far worse than what they accuse you of. Think the worst of yourself and the best of others, for no one is weaker or more fallen than you. In this way you will always remain in a humble frame of mind and feel yourself fully dependent on My mercy. You will be unaffected by idle talk and even outrageous slander. Moreover, you will experience the great benefit and peace of turning to Me alone for consolation and not to the opinions of ordinary mortals.

How can you have peace if you are subject to the whims of capricious men, who are but dolls in the hands of the material energy? Whatever they say or think does not in the least change what you are. You are what you are, not what they say you are. Verily, I see you as you are, not as you or they imagine you to be. True glory and peace come from My satisfaction, not the opinions of others. If you neither hanker for the approval of men, nor fear their displeasure in the execution of your service, you will enjoy great and lasting peace. Anxiety, undue concern, mental anguish, fear, and therefore distraction of the mind and senses all come from illusion and misplaced love. Love Me alone and live in the sunlight of Krishna consciousness; then all bad elements will flee, just as darkness flees before the rising sun.

THE SOUL: Blessed is Your Holy Name, My Lord, and great and wondrous are Your ways. In infinite wisdom You allow me to be tempted and to suffer the results of sinful activities just to reprove and correct my waywardness. How kind You are not to allow me to go on forever in my rebellion! Being a loving Father, You chastise me for my own good.

But this present difficulty, my Master, seems more than I can bear. It is sorely afflicting my spirit. I am weighted down in heaviness, not knowing what to do. Help me, my Lord. I have no place to turn but to You. Lord Hari, You who take away everything from Your devotee, take away my false pride and self-satisfaction, that You alone may be glorified through me. Be pleased, O Krishna, to deliver me from this vain imagination, and establish me in the eternal freedom of devotional service. I have no good qualification and I am most wretched, but You, my Lord, are an ocean of mercy and the Savior of the most fallen. Have pity on this fallen soul. Without You, I am lost.

What more can I say? You are Supreme and independent, and You can do whatever You like. Who can question You, or call You to account? You are completely free to do anything and everything. Therefore let my only prayer be, "Thy will be done. Thy will be done." Whether I am in sickness or health, in happiness or distress, in temptation or consolation, Your desire is best. Give me that awareness at every hour of every day. Let me bear every difficulty with gladness. Grant me the patience to endure to the end.

✩✩✩✩✩✩✩✩✩✩✩✩✩✩✩✩✩

Meditation 67

Krishna Is Our Eternal Friend

THE LORD IN THE HEART: Do not be troubled and do not be afraid. I am your eternal Friend and will never leave you or forsake you. When you are sorely tested and deeply troubled, come to Me, open your heart and reveal your mind. Your hesitation in turning to Me and depending on My grace is your greatest impediment to advancement in Krishna consciousness. Frequently, you try to take shelter of worldly comforts and sense pleasure, and only when you are frustrated by these do you turn to Me. Now let Me be your first refuge and your principal defense. Know that I am the swift Deliverer of those who put their faith in Me. Furthermore, apart from Me, there is no protection from the illusion of *maya*.

Stand firm and take courage. Grow strong in divine grace by My mercy. Even if you sometimes suffer weariness or even reverses, have faith in Me. I am very near and am able to give you complete protection. Whatever has been lost, I am able to restore again in full measure; indeed, I will restore it heaped up and spilling over. I am not poor or miserly; what I have promised, I will surely deliver. Get up and fight manfully, to the death if need be. Be valiant and brave, and always expect My help. Have faith. Wait patiently, and I will come to aid you.

All of your problems are simply creations of the mind—a tempting thought or a baseless fear. Why worry about the future? The present is peaceful, but you miss it by your undue concern for tomorrow. "Sufficient unto the day is the evil thereof." How foolish you are to grieve or rejoice over things that are no more substantial than dreams, things that may never come to pass. This is the working of *maya*, My illusory energy, that deludes the conditioned soul and takes away this golden opportunity to develop love for Me. Whether the mind is diverted by love of the present or fear of the future, the result is the same: *maya* has prevented you from thinking of Me. Therefore, do not be deceived. Always think of Me in My beautiful, original form of Krishna, playing a flute and enchanting all who listen to My transcendental song.

Why should your heart be troubled, and why should you be afraid? Do you think that I am far away? I am closer than the air you breathe and more ready to help than you can imagine. Why do you think that all is lost just because things go contrary to your understanding? Judge not according to human calculations, but accept the judgment of the scriptures and saintly teachers. Nor should you feel forsaken in times of hardship and difficulty. Since it is all My plan for your ultimate purification, it is best for you. Just as gold becomes more valuable when tried in fire, My devotee shines more brilliantly when proved by adversity. I know the secrets of your heart, and I know what will bring you to perfection. Indeed, I know everything; but Me, no one knows. Have faith in Me, My child, and trust in My ways.

Do not be puffed up, thinking yourself to be what you are not. You are My eternal part and parcel. You can do nothing alone, but only what I allow. What I give, I can take away and restore if I desire. Before I give it, it is Mine, and after I give it, it remains Mine. Thus, in fact, I take nothing away that is not Mine. Nor can you renounce anything but what is already Mine, for everything comes from Me.

Moreover, you should be peaceful in all conditions. What appears to be adversity today will be joy tomorrow if you see it as coming from Me; and what is happiness today will become exceedingly bitter if I do not sanction it. If you surrender to Me and follow My instructions, you will never be dejected or confused in any circumstance, but you will realize everything to be My loving kindness. I have promised you not a life of ease but one of struggle, not material honor but worldly contempt, not idleness but a labor of love. Remember these things, My child, ponder them in your heart continuously, and you will reap the greatest harvest—My eternal love.

☆☆☆☆☆☆☆☆☆☆☆☆☆☆

Meditation 68

Seek The Creator, Not The Creation

THE SOUL: Without special mercy, my Lord, I will never be indifferent to material conditions. At the same time, as long as I am influenced by externals, I am not free and cannot completely take shelter of Your Lotus Feet. What shelter in the shade of Your Lotus Feet! What sweetness and satisfaction! That relief is never available to one who seeks anything apart from You. How free is he who desires neither heaven nor earth but only You, my Lord!

Mental speculators, seeking You in the world of phenomena, are forced to confess, "Not this, not this." They may even push their nose and stand on their head and claim, "I am moving the sun, I am moving the moon, I am God," but the next moment they run to the dentist to relieve a toothache. Although You appear in human form as You desire, You are not ordinary, nor are You a common living being. No one is equal to You, neither now nor after so-called liberation. Still, You reside in the hearts of all and are even within and between the countless trillions of atoms. You are never visible to the foolish and envious, but You gladly appear in Your original form of Shyamasundara before those whose eyes are anointed with the balm of love. Such love, however, must be exclusive: love of God and love of the world cannot coexist, not even for a second. As soon as we look to earthly things, the eye of spiritual vision is darkened. If we cannot see Your eternal form of bliss, it is because we have not totally, utterly separated ourselves from transitory sense objects.

For this, Your divine help is required. To lift the soul above its limited conception of self to the unlimited realization of simultaneous oneness and difference with You, we must understand that we are eternally one with You in quality, but minute in quantity. Unless we are elevated in consciousness, free from material desire and entirely surrendered to You, all our possessions and endeavors are of little value. If we think there is anything great save You, either in the worlds above or below, then we are doomed to enter again into a mother's womb for another term of imprisonment in this material world. After many, many births and deaths, we will come to know that there is nothing apart from You and that You are everything. Then we will want to surrender to You.

There is a vast difference between the perfect knowledge of an enlightened devotee and the learning of a mundane scholar, however brilliant and erudite he may be. Knowledge that comes from above is free from human defect and freely given. It leads always upward, whereas material education, acquired only after hard labor, is unstable, imperfect, and lost with the change of body. Those who are wise and never deceived always seek the higher path, not the freeway to hell.

There are many who profess zeal for spiritual life but do not care for the discipline required. Nor do they have a taste for self-mortification

and an abhorrence of sense gratification. Of what use is a show of goodness and godliness if inside we are full of abominations like lust, anger,
and greed? We spend all our time and money on ephemeral things and
seldom have any for serving the eternal. After only a little struggle we
falter, not considering the deadly reactions of our deeds. We are not
careful about to whom or what we give our first love, nor do we feel
remorse for our transgressions and omissions. Alas, what fools we mortals be! Who will deliver us from the wrath to come?

God is not mocked. What a man sows, he also reaps. If we pit ourselves against You, dear Krishna, we will suffer the same fate as Ravana
and Kamsa. If we chant Your Holy Name and purify our existence, we
will gain inner strength and manifest the fruits of a holy life, as so many
great devotees throughout the ages have.

Unfortunately, people in general are not much interested in goodness
but in material success. A man is judged not by his spiritual virtues
but by his mundane accomplishments. What is his bank balance? To
which club does he belong? Is he wealthy or famous? Is he a well-known
playwright or a famous performer? Few care whether he is humble in
spirit or patient in discharging his duty. Few ask if he is a soul surrendered to God and compassionate to all living entities. Truly, man looks
to the outward appearance; You, Lord, look to the heart. One way leads
to illusion and ignorance; the other, to Truth and fullness of life. Keep
me on the right side, my Lord.

☆☆☆☆☆☆☆☆☆☆☆☆☆☆

Meditation 69

Renunciation And Penance

THE LORD IN THE HEART: Consider this proverb, My child: "He who loses himself for My sake finds himself, but he who keeps himself loses all that he has." You will never be perfect or free until you renounce everything for Me. Those who try to enjoy themselves are bound up again and again in an unbroken chain of desire. Become free by following the regulative principles of freedom and relish My unbounded mercy by unconditional surrender. If you resist Me, I will still control you, but through My inferior, material nature. Thus you will act, impelled by the three modes—goodness, passion and ignorance—and you will always be disturbed by their reactions, birth after birth. If you are driven by curiosity and envy, looking for comfort rather than My service, your quest for happiness is sure to be frustrated, for whatever is not rooted in Me must fail.

Save yourself by following My wise counsel: "Abandon all material conceptions, and just surrender to Me. I will give you complete protection. Do not fear." Keep these words in your heart, My child, and put them into practice; then you will find perfect peace.

THE SOUL: But that is very hard, my Lord, and cannot be accomplished even after many lifetimes. If I could follow that one instruction, I would be perfect.

THE LORD IN THE HEART: Don't be afraid of the perfect path, My child. Such a chance is rarely achieved; so press on with the utmost zeal. In this very life, you can attain the heights of Krishna consciousness and return to My eternal abode. As your all-loving Lord and Master, I want this for you more than you do yourself. When you approach pure love for Me, you will have no thought of anything but Me. This will greatly satisfy Me, and when I am satisfied, you will feel the greatest peace and joy. But since you are still immature, you must learn much and give up many things that you are presently attached to. Abandon everything for Me, and all your desires will be fulfilled.

Why should you take counsel of the wicked or put your faith in riches that perish with the setting of the sun? Rather, you should seek the treasure of transcendental wisdom, which renders even the rarest gifts of this world pale and insignificant. Therefore, put aside all earthly things and enjoy the pleasures of paradise in association with Me. This, My friend, is your original blissful nature for which you have been searching since time immemorial.

If I ask you to exchange what is valuable for what is contemptible, you should immediately do it. Your vision is imperfect, but Mine is perfect. Your desire is limited; Mine, absolute. Have faith in Me, for I want to give you the greatest gift. Even if mean men do not understand the worth of humility and self-denial, you, My son, should, for I have placed all things before you for your understanding. Men may praise devotional life with their mouths, but their lives hardly show it. Following their own whims born of unlimited lusty desires, they gradually descend to the lowest species. Do not follow them, but follow in the footsteps of pure devotees who have sacrificed everything to gain Me. It is said that one should sell all that he has to buy the pearl of infinite value. I am that pearl, which is hidden from many but offered to you. Will you pay the price?

☆☆☆☆☆☆☆☆☆☆☆☆☆☆

Meditation 70

Steadiness Is More Important Than Excitement

THE LORD IN THE HEART: Trust not in the emotions of the mind and senses, O little one, for they go one way today and another tomorrow. To be in a material body means to be subject to change. First, you are born, then you grow, you remain for some time, produce some byproducts, and finally dwindle and vanish. Vanity of vanity, all is vanity. This world is not false, as some philosophers contend, but endlessly mutable. As long as you remain within the material world, you will experience one change after another, whether you like it or not. There will be times of merriment and times of sadness, times of peacefulness and times of tribulation, times of devotional fervor and times of laxity, times of activity and times of rest, times of gravity and times of frivolity. One who is wise, My son, knows these changes to be the workings of *maya*, the modes of material nature. They pertain to the material body only, not the spirit soul. The soul, who is eternal and changeless, stands always above these. Therefore, take no thought for the feelings of the body, but think of the soul and its relationship to Me. Being fickle, the mind can carry away the senses even of an intelligent man who is striving for perfection. Be fixed and immovable in your determination, undivided and unchanging in your resolution, and single-minded in your purpose. Then you will attain your desired goal very soon.

I am easily won by those who seek Me with their whole heart. Indeed, it is in exact proportion to their desire that I am attained. Thus one man sees Me in part, and another to a greater degree, but I can be seen as I am only by My pure devotee who has surrendered everything to Me.

Love Me with all your heart, and follow Me wherever I go. Let not your devotion become slack nor your fervor cooled. Many quickly lose their purity of intention, being again attracted by the pleasures of the flesh, the wiles of My external nature. How rare it is to find a soul not allured by these things, completely free from even a tinge of self-seeking! Even the great philosophers and sages want to merge into My existence. This is just a higher form of sense gratification. The expert yogis want mystic benedictions, but this desire is also material. Only My pure devotees are free from all material desires, for they want Me alone. And thus I give Myself to them alone.

Let your intentions be for Me only. One who is divided in his desires is always unstable, and the mind attached to sense gratification lacks the resolution necessary for pure devotional service. Therefore, whatever you do, whatever you eat, whatever charitable activities you perform—do it for My satisfaction. That is action in accordance with the greatest knowledge of all.

☆☆☆☆☆☆☆☆☆☆☆☆☆

Meditation 71

God's Sweetness Is Perceived In Proportion To Our Love

THE SOUL: O Lord, You are my Master, my God, and my Friend. You watch over me and comfort me like a concerned mother and a loving father. What more could my heart desire, my Lord? What greater blessedness is there? O sweet and satisfying thought! To rest in You, to yield to Your desire and fulfill Your every wish! How satisfying to those who love You, but incomprehensible to those envious of You or attached to worldly enjoyment!

Krishna, You are my all in all. Life has no meaning without You. This body and all that is connected to it are Yours. These words of love are blessed to one who understands, and he relishes repeating them over and over. Sweeter still is Your Holy Name, for You are personally present on the tongue of one who sincerely utters that sound.

Ah, Krishna! Krishna! That sound is enough to put to flight all the demons of material desire. By Your presence in that holy sound vibration, You sanctify and beautify all things. Without You, even the most honored things of this world are but loathsome, empty shadows. Men make plans and hold peace conferences, but they cannot secure peace. They manufacture tranquilizers, but they cannot make the heart serene. They hold fairs and festivals and sell fun by the pound, but they cannot bestow real and lasting joy or contentment to the soul. Without You, my Lord, no one can be happy, and no earthly pleasure can long endure. Yet, one who knows Your grace and is blessed by Your mercy can never be unhappy in any condition.

Let my lips sing Your praise and my heart meditate on Your transcendental form. If only I could see without interruption that moonlike face! How unfortunate are the philosophers and so-called wise men who do not know that form of incomparable beauty! Being full of their own vanity and attached to their own putrid flesh, they lack the spiritual eyes to see You. Protect me, O Krishna, from false pride and conceit. Help me to hate every material allurement and to mortify the senses, utilizing them only in relationship to You. Then I will be wise and know that I am Your eternal servant. Give me the eyes to see all things good and to know that they proceed from and exist for You, the All Good. Make me ever mindful of the difference between You, the Cause of all causes, the Creator of everything, and the effect, the created.

O Light of all lights, more brilliant than millions of blazing suns, how unfortunate are those who see only the dazzling effulgence that covers Your real form of eternity, knowledge, and bliss! Shine in my darkened heart and enlighten my being with that knowledge by which all ignorance is destroyed. Awaken my soul to its real powers in devotional service so that I may cling to You alone in the ecstasy of pure love. O Krishna, when will I no longer have separate desires and interests? When will I desire only You and Your desire? When will I be so filled with joy by the chanting of Your Holy Name that the hairs of my body stand on end, and I laugh and cry like a madman, not considering time or place? When will I relish Your presence and make Your pleasure my all in all?

Alas, this flesh clings to me, and illusion engulfs me. I am still tightly bound by the modes of nature. Lust attacks me. I am bewildered by *maya's* temptations. No one can save me but You. Be merciful to me, my Lord. You saved Prahlad from his demonic father, Hiranyakasipu. You granted Dhruva his heart's desire. For You, nothing is difficult. You can do anything. O God, my only refuge in time of trouble, do You not also hear my prayer? I do not ask for material benedictions like wealth and power, nor even for spiritual advancement or higher consciousness. I am begging You for something far more rare and difficult to achieve—complete and perfect surrender to Your Lotus Feet. This is my only prayer.

☆☆☆☆☆☆☆☆☆☆☆☆☆☆

Meditation 72

The Embodied Soul Must Ever Be Tested

THE LORD IN THE HEART: Just when you think you are most secure, My child, you are being most severely tested. If anyone in this world thinks that he is free from temptation, he is already deluded by *maya*. Be strong in the Lord and arm yourself with the weapon of knowledge. Your enemies are all about and seek to destroy you from all sides. Guard yourself diligently on the right by following the regulative principles of Krishna consciousness, and on the left by having faith in My special mercy. Guard yourself in front by patiently waiting upon My desire, and in back by remembering My glorious pastimes and activities. In this way you will eliminate all foes and easily cross over the terrible ocean of birth and death.

If you do not always think of Me by meditating on My transcendental form and chanting My Holy Name, willing to sacrifice everything to satisfy My desire, you will not be able to withstand the weapons of *maya*. Wounded by her burning arrows of doubt and discouragement, many great warriors have already left the fight in disgrace, failing to win the crown of glory awaiting those who persevere to the end. Put on the invincible armor of transcendental sound and triumphantly pass through the midst of your enemies. Although I have already slain them from eternity past, I want you to oppose them manfully and win the praise of all. Verily, I take more pleasure in seeing My devotee honored than in being honored Myself. Now stand and fight. Victory and opulence are yours for certain. Inaction is a sign of laziness and cowardice, contrary to My order and inauspicious in every way.

If you seek a life of perpetual happiness here on earth, how will you ever attain an eternal life of unending bliss in My Kingdom? Look not for your comfort in this world, where miseries strike at every turn, but prepare yourself with great patience for the blessedness of life with Me in My spiritual abode. Seek My peace in the Vaikuntha sky, where birth and death and the influence of time are conspicuous by their absence. Do not expect peace among men and nations, for they will never be at peace. For the sake of My love, you should gladly tolerate all things, even suffering and sorrow, testing and tribulation, harassment and humiliation. Then you will be known as My faithful disciple. Blessed are you, My child, for hardships lead to virtue for my devotees but to frustration and rebellion for those who envy Me. Indeed, hardships form a crown of jewels on the heads of My surrendered souls. Who is so foolish that he will not endure a little hardship now, for a few short days, in order to gain everlasting glory and My eternal favor?

But now is the time of hard labor and arduous endeavor. You must strive upward and onward along the path that the saints have trod. Do not expect the road to be always smooth, and do not wish to be always consoled. It was not easy for the holy ones of old. Indeed, I often afflicted and severely tried them in order to reveal their greatness and unalloyed devotion to Me. They are remembered today because they accepted all difficulties as My mercy and bore them most patiently. Having full confidence in Me and none in themselves, they proved their faith and passed from the mortal sufferings of this world to the bliss and glory of My eternal abode. Do you expect to enjoy immediately what is usually attained only after long purification of the soul by severe penance and austerity? No, My child, you too must purify your existence, shedding many tears while seeking Me with all your heart.

Now, My little one, you must learn to wait patiently upon Me, for patience is the symptom of surrender. The desire to serve is also service. Rest assured that in due course I will reveal My plan to you, and then you can act for Me with all your might. Be courageous and do not lose heart. Do not look back, but serve Me enthusiastically with your body, mind, and words. Trust in Me, and I will reward you abundantly. Nothing is difficult for Me, and I am with you always.

☆☆☆☆☆☆☆☆☆☆☆☆☆☆

Meditation 73

The Dogs Bark, The Caravan Passes

THE LORD IN THE HEART: Have firm faith in My words, O little one, and trust in My direction. Neglect the counsel of the ungodly, and care not for their opinions. Know what is good and true from the holy scriptures and the teachings of My pure devotees. Mental speculation and mundane experience never reveal the ways of peace, but My words bring perfect peace from all material miseries. Thus you should tolerate the rantings of the mad materialists and cheerfully accept all harassments with a humble heart that cares only for My satisfaction. Put faith neither in others, who are by nature fickle, nor in your own deluded self, but place all your trust in Me, for I swiftly deliver My devotee from the ocean of birth and death.

Try as you like, you will not be able to satisfy all men. Even Lord Nityananda, who desired to bless every living entity with the mercy of Lord Chaitanya, could not please the sinful Jagai and Madhai. Those in the modes of passion and ignorance do not know what is to be done and not done, and they mistake irreligion for religion and religion for irreligion. They do not appreciate your attempts to save them from the hellish life that awaits them, and they misjudge and despise your charity. Still, you should endeavor on My behalf to turn them from their sinful ways. Thus you will show your great compassion and true love for all beings.

Commit all things to Me, and depend on My mercy. I see all and know all and will surely give you full protection. Let humility and patience be your emblem so that malicious tongues and foolish accusations will not affect you. Stand on My instruction, and you will be secure in every situation.

Why should you fear mere mortal man? Who is he that you tremble at his command? Is he any different than the grass, which grows and is cut down and cast into the fire? Time I am, destroyer of all. Because of Me the wind blows, the sun rises, and the moon sheds her cooling rays. Remember Me and you will never fear My insignificant creature. After all, what can he do to you, who are spirit soul? His words and fury cannot touch the soul who rests in Me, but he does himself very great harm. An offense at the feet of My pure devotee is more painful to Me than a thousand arrows in My side. Such an offender will never escape My wrath, even if he be king of the world.

Thus you should never become impatient or disheartened, even when it appears that you are dishonored or defeated. Do not lament, and do not waver in your determination to attain pure love for Me, the real goal of life. Rather, look to Me, and think of Me in My beautiful form of

Krishna, standing in a three-curved bending stance. Chant My Name, and call upon Me, for I am very near and anxious to help. I have all power and can immediately deliver you from all distressful conditions. Do not fear, My child. I am here.

☆☆☆☆☆☆☆☆☆☆☆☆☆☆

Meditation 74

What Do You Have To Renounce?

THE LORD IN THE HEART: My foolish child, why do you try to hang on to the very thing that is the source of your troubles? Give up your selfishness and realize your true self-interest in Me. Identifying oneself with the temporary body and its possessions is always demeaning to the soul. Truly, it is the cause of all suffering in this world. Renounce self-will, and find self-fulfillment in Me.

THE SOUL: I have often tried to do that, my Lord. How long shall I go on trying? Seven times? Or seventy? Or is there another means that brings quicker results?

THE LORD IN THE HEART: You must try again and again, like a child learning to walk. Neither seven or seventy has any meaning. You must endeavor until you attain success, and that success will come when you resign yourself to Me utterly—in every way, at every hour, in matters great and small. Nothing is beyond My purview or jurisdiction. When you are actually in transcendental knowledge, you will not see anything as separate from Me. Rather, you will see yourself as My subordinate part. When you are thus freed from self-delusion, you will engage in My eternal loving service. How else could you ever be Mine, or I yours? As two lovers become one in desire, so you must unite with Me in eternal loving service. Both your inner and outer life will benefit greatly, for I am good in every way. The sooner you surrender to Me, the quicker you will feel relief. The more sincerely and completely you surrender, the more you will feel the reciprocation of My love.

In whatever way one approaches Me, I reward him accordingly. Some profess great asceticism and renunciation, but they hedge it about with many conditions and reservations. Not having full faith and confidence in Me, they want to make arrangements to protect their own interest. I am sorry to say that they can never experience My presence very deeply. There are others who enter into My service very enthusiastically, offering to surrender everything to Me, but after some time, being assailed by the temptations of *maya*, they fall down from their high position. Like dogs returning to their vomit, these unfortunate souls again take to the foolishness of sense gratification, chewing the chewed, birth after birth. Blessed is he who presses on to the goal and never looks back, for he verily reaches My abode in due course of time. There, in My association, he gains the true liberty of My devotees and enjoys their blissful friendship. Therefore, you must daily renounce the comforts of this world, and sacrifice all for My satisfaction. Without such sacrifice, no loving union can endure.

On the other hand, you must be careful not to think, "I have given up so much for the service of the Lord." From My point of view, you possess nothing to give up. I create everything, I maintain everything, and, when I desire, I destroy everything. Whatever exists is nothing but a transformation of My energy. It was Mine in the past, it is Mine now, and it will always be Mine. What, then, do you have to renounce, foolish creature? At most, you can renounce your false claim to My property, which gives you the distinction of no longer being a thief. Beware of false pride.

I have frequently reminded you to think of Me and become My devotee. Forsake your independent ways and submit to My protection. That will bring you great joy and lasting peace. Absorb yourself in giving rather than getting, for it is more satisfying to give than to receive. Ask, "How can I serve You?" and expect nothing in return. Depend on Me only, and trust Me with all your heart, and verily I will become yours. Thus your heart will be light, and darkness will find no place in you.

Everything is situated on desire, and I am fulfilling everyone's desires since time immemorial. Strive diligently with undaunted determination to end all selfishness, and desire nothing other than what I desire for you. Then you will surely attain success. To die to self means to live with Me forevermore. In My abode there are no vain imaginations, worldly disturbances, material miseries, or worrisome cares. My spiritual habitation is eternal, full of knowledge and bliss, and free from all inebriety. There is no fear or death—only pure, unalloyed love for Me.

Why do you hesitate and doubt? I am your eternal friend and ever well-wisher. Come home, My child, come home.

☆☆☆☆☆☆☆☆☆☆☆☆☆☆

Meditation 75

Right Living Makes For Right Perception

THE LORD IN THE HEART: You are meant to be free, My child, as free as the wind and the lilies of the field, but such freedom is never enjoyed by those who are enslaved by passion or immersed in ignorance. To control every outward act and endeavor, you must strive manfully to conquer the unbridled senses and mind and make them subject to your command. Thus you will be their master, not their slave. My servants are free, for they labor out of love, and no force from above or below can dissuade them from their chosen course.

Do not confuse freedom with licentiousness, however, for the man of no restraint is bound hand and foot by his uncontrolled senses. Ask the drunkard to forgo his glass of wine, or the woman-hunter his prostitute. They are driven by insatiable lust, even against their self interest. But My devotees are free indeed, for they follow the regulative principles of freedom and thereby gain My limitless mercy. They care not for temporal things, although they know how to use everything in My service. In this way, with their feet on the ground and their vision fixed on Me, they easily pass through this world to the next.

Therefore, standing always above the world of here and now, contemplate what is to come, not in time but beyond time, in My abode where there is neither birth nor death and where all things are eternal and full of knowledge and bliss. And contemplate Me as the Supreme Controller, for all things are ordered by Me and exist for My pleasure.

Such contemplation, if it be simple and pure, will lead you to reject the outward appearance, seen with the physical eye and heard with the physical ear, and to perceive directly, with spiritual senses, the Absolute Truth, the Supreme Personality of Godhead, Lord Krishna, who is eternally playing His flute and sporting in the groves of Vrindaban. I am that selfsame Lord, waiting for you to turn to Me and heed My instructions given for your welfare. Whatever you want can be found in Me. What do you need? Protection? Support? Knowledge? Friendship and love? Pure devotional service? Freedom from doubt? No one can give more than I, for no one possesses more than I. Take refuge of Me in the secret chamber of your heart. Ask of Me whatever you will, and I will surely give it.

Trust not to your own understanding, but in all things acknowledge Me, and I will show you the way. Listen carefully to My voice and to the voice of My representative, the bona fide spiritual master, who repeats My message. Trust not in the fair words of flatterers nor in the advice of mental speculators, for they will deceive you by their showbottle devotion. Know the sound of Truth, and let that sound guide you always. Surrender to Me, bow down to Me, and become My devotee. Thus you will come to Me. I promise you this, for you are very dear to Me.

☆☆☆☆☆☆☆☆☆☆☆☆☆☆☆☆☆

Meditation 76

Take No Thought For Tomorrow

THE LORD IN THE HEART: If you put your trust in Me, My little one, I will certainly do what is best for you and watch over your every concern. Be patient, and in time you will see that My arrangements are perfect and bring about good for all.

THE SOUL: O Krishna, I know that You are all good and perfect in every way. I also know that my own perceptions and desires are distorted by illusion and that I do not even know what to ask for. I can understand that I should surrender to Your will and commit my life wholly to Your care, yet this seems most difficult. Greed for enjoying the present and worry for the future are so ingrained in me that it is almost impossible to offer myself for Your service without reservation. Help me, O Lord.

THE LORD IN THE HEART: It is a fact, My dear one, that undue concern for the future is very detrimental to peace and tranquility, for real happiness is always found in the present. In My abode there is neither past nor future, but all exists as it is eternally. You, My child, are also eternal. Past and future exist only in relation to this body which you presently inhabit. But this body is not you. You are the spirit soul, whose presence is seen in the consciousness spread all over the body.

It is *maya's* trick that makes you identify yourself with this body and thereby undergo the chain of actions and reactions that causes repeated birth and death. But self-realization, recognition of your true nature as spirit soul, breaks the fetters of illusion forever.

Be watchful, My child, and let not this illusion ensnare you again. Listen neither to the undisciplined mind nor to the agitated senses, for they create a maze of desires leading to death. How often have you ardently sought to fulfill some desire, only to find, after attaining it, that it was not what you thought it would be? The mind, always restless, flits from one sense object to another, dragging the conditioned soul here and there with no profit. Be wise, and learn to desire only what is good and profitable for you as a spirit soul.

Progress should be measured in terms of spiritual realization, which brings real freedom and eternal security. Progress should never be thought of as economic development or so-called scientific advancement. Scientific and economic progress are simply other names for material bondage, because they prepare one for rebirth in this mortal world. The progress of the soul consists of self-denial and self-awareness. By denying the material, you become aware of the eternal. And know that I am the Supreme Eternal. But you can never have both this temporary world and Me simultaneously, for you will be devoted either to the one or to the other.

The illusions of this world are ever present, and as long as you identify yourself with this body, you will be subject to temptation day and night. These are tests allowed by Me to separate the sheep from the goats, the devotees from the pretenders and imposters. Those who succumb to *maya's* call descend into lower and lower species of life, but My devotees, by heeding My voice, are guided back home, back to Godhead, to live with Me eternally.

✩✩✩✩✩✩✩✩✩✩✩✩✩✩✩✩

Meditation 77

There Is Nothing Good In Me

THE SOUL: O my God, Lord of the universe, Savior of the fallen! When I think of Your greatness, I am overcome with ecstasy, and my mind reels from incomprehension. What am I in comparison to You? I am not even a grain of sand or a speck in the vast ocean of cosmic creation. How is it possible that You have bestowed Your grace upon me again and again? If You should ignore me or crush me in the process of executing Your mighty deeds, I could not complain. Nor dare I think that You should come when I call and do whatever I desire, for You are inconceivable in every way and powerful beyond imagination. When I consider myself, I must admit that I am nothing and by my own efforts can do nothing good. I lack even the knowledge to know the proper course of action. I am deficient in all things, and even my natural inclination is void of truth. Without Your help, my Lord, without being uplifted and infused by Your grace, I have no function or purpose.

How different I am from You, my Lord! I tend to become lax and half-hearted in my commitment, whereas You are eternally fixed in goodness, justice, holiness, and love. Even now, I am as apt to go backward as forward and to change from day to day like the weather. My mind is most unsteady until I think of You and chant the glories of Your

Holy Name and uncommon activities. Then, like a loving Friend, you extend Your almighty hand and guide me onward and upward to Your own abode. By thinking of You and hearing those transcendental sounds, my stonelike heart is softened and convinced to rest in You alone.

Finding satisfaction only in You, I no longer seek worldly association for sense gratification but aspire to become perfect in the service of even the least of Your servants. Indeed, You are more pleased by sincere service to Your devotee than service offered directly to You. Who can understand such greatness? What love for Your devotee! I have heard from great authorities that You take more pleasure in becoming a Friend, Son, or Lover to Your devotee than in being the Lord of Vaikuntha.

Thank You, dear Krishna, for acknowledging me and placing me as one of the atoms at Your Lotus Feet. To You, I must be nothing but a bother—vain, weak, and unstable. Yet You have loved me and accompanied me birth after birth to lead me back home. There is no room for self-glory or the desire to be highly esteemed. Indeed, self-glory is the greatest plague and the most vile obstacle, drawing me away from You and thus robbing me of my true glory and divine grace. When I hanker for worldly honor, my soul is debased; when I am proud of myself, You are most displeased.

Therefore, let me pursue the only true glory, the sound of Your Holy Name and the service of Your Lotus Feet. Let Your qualities be praised, not mine. Let Your pastimes be magnified, not mine. Let Your fame spread to every town and village, but let me remain Your unknown slave. Let others seek another joy, but I want only what comes from You. You are the joy of my heart and my only glory. Human honor and fame and power—everything within the material creation—is empty and foolish compared to Your eternal, inconceivable opulence in the Spiritual Sky. You possess wealth, fame, beauty, knowledge, strength, and renunciation, simultaneously and unlimitedly, and thus Your everlasting glory is heralded throughout the countless ages of time and eternity. Let me also go on extolling Your praises, singing this song of eternal love, forever and ever, world without end.

☆☆☆☆☆☆☆☆☆☆☆☆☆☆

Meditation 78

Despise What Is Material

THE LORD IN THE HEART: I advise you, My son, to honor others but expect no honor in return, to see others as elevated in Krishna consciousness, but yourself as lower than the straw in the street. Despise yourself and walk humbly in My ways. Lift up your voice and cry to Me, chanting My Holy Name, and the miseries of material life will not be able to affect you. As the lotus lives within a lake without its leaves touching water, you, by My grace, will pass untouched over the ocean of material existence.

THE SOUL: O Lord, You are my God and Friend. You are always with me, and You see to my every need. Still, I am easily blinded by passion and misled by desire. When I examine myself truthfully, I find no good, although good is about me in everything I see. Your whole creation is perfect and complete: I find no fault or evil in it, save my own causeless unwillingness to surrender to Your Lotus Feet and my own tendency to judge things with conditioned senses. You are perfect in all You do, and there is nothing I can justly complain to You about.

But I am such an ungrateful wretch that I cannot appreciate Your mercy and loving kindness. Instead, I often break Your commandments and neglect Your advice. Thus, I have greatly sinned and offended You, and now every creature is rightly enraged with me. If I do not satisfy You, the Soul of all, how can anyone be satisfied with me? You deserve infinite praise and the highest honor and glory, but I, failing to render even a fraction of Your due, have become more abominable than a worm in stool. Completely confused and devoid of all but bestial affections, always frustrated by material nature, and baffled in my attempts to make a happy life of sense enjoyment, I am in great anxiety. In such a hard struggle, how can there be peace and contentment?

THE LORD IN THE HEART: You are right, My child. There is no peace and happiness in material life. Nor can you find inner strength and spiritual enlightenment apart from Me. If you seek shelter in the company of any creature or in the enjoyment of anything not related to Me, you will be frustrated and unhappy. You will also become entangled in the laws of *karma*, for every action has a reaction, either good or evil. But if you surrender to Me and take shelter of Me alone, you will abide in everlasting Truth and remain free from all reactions. In this way you will pass beyond the region of birth and death in full realization of the eternity of the soul. You will not grieve for the death of even your most near and dear friend, knowing that it is only the material body that is subject to destruction. For the soul, there is never birth nor death, nor having once been, does he ever cease to be. It is the soul you love, not the body, and the soul is My part and parcel. The love you feel for your friend is really meant for Me.

Whatever lovable qualities attract you to others are really Mine, for I am the Reservoir of all lovable qualities. Without Me, love is lust, and no relationship can endure or have meaning. Therefore, make Me the center, and your love will be true and pure.

Sometimes those who are yet weak and immature take this to mean that the friendship of men is evil and must be given up. That is wrong. Only the fellowship of worldly men should be given up. The association of My devotees is very beneficial. You will draw near to Me and develop attachment to devotional service in exact proportion to your giving up sense gratification. Mere abstention from undesirable activity is not enough. There must be positive engagement to replace it. Attachment to Me is worth far more than simple detachment from matter, for without the positive attraction of the spirit, there is every chance that you will again fall down to enjoy the base pleasures of the flesh. Therefore, be wary of the vile material nature that now entraps you, and meditate on the all-blissful spiritual nature of which you are a part.

Attribute all good to Me, not to yourself, and let My goodness be manifest in you always. By My grace this is possible when you empty yourself of all other loves. I enter into the heart entirely devoted to Me and fill it with divine grace. Thus, ecstatic love immediately manifests. But if you look to even the smallest creature, you will not be able to see Me. Your love must be for Me alone. Then I will make all things known to you, and you will know Me as I am, even as you are known to Me.

☆☆☆☆☆☆☆☆☆☆☆☆☆

Meditation 79

Speculative Knowledge Is Of No Avail

THE LORD IN THE HEART: Dear little one, don't be affected by the flowery words and high-sounding philosophy of mental speculators. Spirituality consists not of dry arguments but of realization achieved through a life of holiness and surrender. In one who follows My instructions, which enliven the soul and enlighten the mind, a change of heart is wrought. In that state, one feels genuine repentance and ecstatic love for Me. What is the use of falsely pretending to know the scriptures or to be advanced in Krishna consciousness if your heart is full of lust, anger, and greed? Religiousness in name alone cannot bring about a revolution in consciousness. It is rather a disturbance to the society of genuine devotees. Thus, if you wish to be My faithful disciple, you must purify yourself from all unwanted habits and become clean within and without. Freedom from sinful activities is far more important than erudition in holy books or pedantic explanations to perplexing questions.

However well taught and scholarly you become from cultivating knowledge for many lifetimes, you will eventually have to realize that I am the Source and end of all learning. Therefore, My little one, it is best to surrender to Me immediately. Put all your faith in Me, and I will reveal all things to you in due course of time. It is not to scholarship that I am attracted but to purity of heart and humility of spirit. Just try to understand Me by approaching My pure devotee and inquiring with true submission and service. My devotees know Me best and are very anxious to give that knowledge to others. Thus knowing Me, you will become wise and your soul will be satisfied.

But how unfortunate are those who, neglecting the opportunity for self-realization afforded by human life, waste their time pursuing mundane profit. The time is near when I will appear and test what you have learned, for at death I scrutinize the deeds of everyone. Then hidden things will be made known, and the foolish arguments of men will be silenced. Blessed are they who know Me, for they will abide in Me always in transcendental peace, relishing pastimes of pleasure and love. But woe to those who are found wanting in knowledge of Me, for they have condemned themselves to a life in the darkest regions of material existence, a life without Me, who am the joy of all.

Take heed to prepare yourself well, My son, for you know not when that hour will come. In the face of death, all material things fade and only I remain. Therefore, store up real knowledge and spiritual treasure against that day of reckoning by hearing submissively from Me and My representative, the spiritual master, who can impart more transcendental knowledge to the humble disciple in a moment than universities ever can. This king of knowledge, which endures beyond time, is freely given to those who are not envious of Me and who are fully surrendered souls.

Thus, you should carefully follow My instructions and learn to despise everything that binds you to material consciousness. Occupy yourself only with that which is conducive to Krishna consciousness. Seek not your present comfort, but seek what is eternal and beneficial to the soul. Shun worldly honors and gladly tolerate slander and abuse. Place all your hopes and desires in Me for My satisfaction, and thus demonstrate your unflinching love for Me above all others. There is no greater gain or treasure than this, the pearl of great price. My advice is to sell all that you have and purchase it while there is time.

☆☆☆☆☆☆☆☆☆☆☆☆☆☆

Meditation 80

All Men Worship Me

THE LORD IN THE HEART: Yes, it is a fact that all men worship Me, but not all with the same intention. Some worship Me for material gain, and some to be seen of men. Some seek a heavenly paradise, while others want to merge into My impersonal nature. In proportion to their surrender, they know Me as I am, in My form of eternity, knowledge, and bliss. Thus, to some I reveal mundane truths, and to others, transcendental gems. For some I am manifest in signs and wonders or mystic powers, but to My pure devotees, I appear in My original form, the sweetest Child of Vrindaban.

Even My transcendental instructions, which are one, are not heard by all men alike, but to each man I appear and fulfill his desire. Thus, I am the Supreme Teacher, the Absolute Truth, the Eternal Divine Person, the Knower of all hearts and minds, the Supreme Doer and Permitter of all acts. I am Krishna, the Opulent One, the Supreme Personality of Godhead, who awards everyone the perfect result.

But you, dear friend, cannot always understand My ways and My thoughts, for they are higher than yours. Therefore, little one, there are many affairs you cannot judge and some you should best remain ignorant of. The great sage Jada Bharat passed his days as if dumb. He neither cared for the opinion of gentle society, nor listened to their idle chatter. It is always profitable to avoid materialistic persons, especially those addicted to sex. Likewise, many quarrels will be averted by refraining from useless arguments. Let your yea's be yea, and your nay's nay. When you are upheld by Me, you need have no fear, for if I be for you, who can be against you?

THE SOUL: You are certainly right, my Lord, but I am weak, and my nature is forgetfulness. Although You, whom even fear personified fears, stand by my side anxious to help, I turn to seek aid and comfort from the enemy. Although the soul is by nature eternal, full of knowledge and bliss, complete and sufficient in himself, I lament even a small material loss. I work hard day and night, like an ass or a horse, for a few morsels of bread, while my soul starves for want of nourishment in communion with You. Matters that are of little or no importance occupy my mind, while the most essential thing is neglected. Instead of thinking of You and chanting Your Holy Name, I remain enslaved by *maya*, pursuing Your external energy in a hard struggle for existence that brings very little reward.

O my Lord, Friend of the soul, have mercy upon me. Without Your divine intervention, I am doomed to remain immersed in this illusory pursuit of happiness, which brings no happiness at all but only frustration and misery. Have mercy upon me and save me, I pray. Pick me up from this ocean of birth and death, and teach me to honor and love You. Engage me in Your devotional service, that I may be free from serving these five ruthless taskmasters, the senses. Purge me of every inordinate desire, that I may desire only what is good and pleasing to You. O Soul of all souls, be merciful to me. Give me the shade of Your Lotus Feet.

☆☆☆☆☆☆☆☆☆☆☆☆☆☆

Meditation 81

Beware Of Materialistic Men

THE SOUL: I need Your help, O Lord, for the assistance of others is no better than the aid of toy soldiers. They give an illusion of security, but such false assurance is worse than none. How often have I foolishly sought protection from such fallible fighters, only to find myself defenseless! On the other hand, I have often found Your causeless mercy when I least expected it, and in ways equally unexpected. Therefore, let me neglect the consolation of men, for in You, dear Krishna, I have found salvation and hope. Holy and blessed is Your Name, and inconceivable are Your plans.

But where is that mortal so strong and steady that he is not easily deceived? Despite all care and precaution, who does not sometimes fall into illusion and doubt? Is there anyone but Your pure devotees? Yet, by Your great mercy, You promise that I cannot fall when I confide in You, my Lord, and seek Your Lotus Feet with a pure heart and an unmotivated spirit. Then, You uphold me with Your everlasting arms.

How unlike mortal man! An ordinary friend remains faithful only up to a point, and then the friendship breaks. Even maternal affection has its limits. But You, my Lord, and You alone are always faithful, even when there is no cause for faithfulness. You are my Friend eternally; the greater the trouble, the more quickly You rescue me.

If only I were wise enough to be ever cognizant of Your infinite protection! No earthly fear could cause me anxiety, nor could mere words disturb my rest. Why do I forget? Why do I rush to take shelter of others? Alas, we may be worshipped by others as gods or demons, but we are nothing more than insignificant slaves, awaiting the call of our wonderful Master.

Why should we not put all our trust in You, O Krishna? No one is equal to or greater than You. You are the Supreme Absolute Truth, which neither deceives nor is deceived. The conditioned soul, however, is full of imperfections and weakness. He is a liar by nature because he lives under the illusion that he is a material body, which he is not. However lofty its literary style or expert its philosophical jugglery, mundane speculation is as useless as reflections on water or herculean endeavors performed in a dream. But how that illusion haunts me and fills me with false images and hopes! Sometimes I become envious of my brothers and speak unjustly, causing them severe pain. O Lord, protect me from this sin, and let me not fall into the hell of faultfinding. Rather, fill me with compassion for the plight of sinful men, and place Your message of transcendent love into my mouth.

How right and peaceful it feels to be silent about the affairs of others, not to hear or speak without discrimination, not to be eager to repeat gossip but to leave rectification to You, the discerner of all hearts, not to be carried away by every fad or craze but to humbly submit all things to You, that You may dispose of them according to Your own good pleasure.

Dear Krishna, help me perform devotional service without considering the gaze of men and without desiring profit and adoration. Help me perform with the greatest diligence all those things that promote devotional enthusiasm and the purification of my life.

Protect me from spiritual pride. How easy it is to fall down from having virtues too well known and overpraised, whereas many have attained Your eternal abode even though their merits were unnoticed during their earthly life. Give me the strength and the determination to fight manfully for Your cause, victorious over every evil foe, so that Your Holy Name may resound from my mouth forevermore.

☆☆☆☆☆☆☆☆☆☆☆☆☆

Meditation 82

Pay No Heed To The Talk Of Men

THE LORD IN THE HEART: Be bold, My child, and trust in Me. Why do you consider the words of men to be more important than Mine? Do their words not fly through the ether as sound without fury? Can they harm even an ant or a mosquito? If indeed you are guilty of their accusations, it is well that you mend your ways, and if you are innocent, think of the merit you acquire by gladly tolerating abuse for My sake. Be thankful that you are required to endure only verbal abuse. In your neophyte stage, you could hardly endure more rigorous assaults.

Why should unimportant matters affect you so deeply? Is it not a sign that your heart is still carnal and that you are more attached to the adoration of men than to what is right? It appears that you do not wish to be criticized for a fault or corrected from wrongdoing. Otherwise, why do you try to cover yourself with so many excuses? Open your mind and scrutinize your heart to see if there is still some attraction for the world and some desire for the praise of men. Those who are truly humble and completely dead to this world's glory are never affected by the condemnation of a fault or by loss of social standing.

Listen attentively, My dear one; My words are not like those of mortal man. Indeed, the words of millions of men taken together cannot be compared to Mine. I am the Original Guru, He whose words are heavy because they are spiritual, without defect, and transcendental to this material sphere. By a word, I create and destroy the whole universe. If all man's malice and abuse were spoken against you at once, what effect would it have if you ignored it or considered it no more important than leaves blowing in the wind? Verily, it could not harm one hair of your body.

Who is easily disturbed by words of disparagement? It is he who does not keep Me before his eyes, he whose heart seeks many loves. However, My devotees, reposing all their affections in Me, are not swayed by the pleadings of the mind and senses, and thus remain free from the bondage of men. My devotees are always protected by My grace and know that I am the Witness of every man's heart and the Knower of all things. I know who causes pain to others and who patiently endures tribulations, and I am the just Judge, discerning the truth and recompensing fairly. It is not for you to say, "Vengeance is Mine. I will repay." Do not try to counter one mean word with another, but tolerate all things for My pleasure. Indeed, My pure devotees realize that it is from Me that harsh words proceed, that according to My infinite wisdom, I allow it. It is not possible to understand the whys and wherefores of your Lord's decisions, but you can humbly surrender in faith and love.

Do not worry, My child: I shall certainly reward all men according to their actions, but in My own time and according to My own good pleasure. Man's testimony is often deceiving, but as I am the Lord in the heart, My judgements are perfect and true. No one can stand against them. These things are hidden from the wise of this world but revealed even to the young and the weak if their hearts are pure. I am never mistaken. I cannot be mistaken, even if all earthly councils and courts disapprove of My judgement.

To Me, therefore—either in My form as Supersoul or in My form as Spiritual Master or in My written word—you ought to submit every decision. Not looking to your own desires or to the opinions of men, you will triumph by My grace even in the most trying circumstances. Just remember that it is I, the best Friend of all living entities, who know the innermost recesses of the heart and the most hidden thoughts of all men. I judge not according to the criteria of imperfect creatures, who see only the outward appearance, but according to the motive of the heart. Thus, many actions that are praised by men are disapproved by Me, and many things approved by Me are condemned by materialistic men.

THE SOUL: O Lord of my heart, You know my hopes and aspirations, my fears and frustrations. You are the righteous Judge and most intimate Friend. You know the ignorance and depravity of the conditioned soul; yet, with infinite strength and patience, You help me always. Infuse me with the power to resist evil and do good, for my own strength is insufficient. My Lord, You know all things, both what I know and do not know. Factually, I do not even know what is good for me; therefore I ought to accept whatever comes as Your special loving mercy for me. Humbly bearing all inconveniences, I should meekly tolerate abuse. Where I have failed in this regard, extend Your mercy in forgiveness and Your grace in endurance. O Krishna, I am Your insignificant servant, full of faults. Grant me Your pardon so that I may try again and again and, by the gradual purification of my soul, slowly but surely reach that golden shore from which we never return to this miserable world of birth and death. There we live eternally with You in transcendental bliss, singing Your glories, and chanting Your Holy Name: Hare Krishna, Hare Krishna, Krishna Krishna, Hare Hare, Hare Rama, Hare Rama, Rama Rama, Hare Hare.

☆☆☆☆☆☆☆☆☆☆☆☆☆

Meditation 83

Bear Up Manfully For Eternal Life

THE LORD IN THE HEART: Little soul, take heart and do not be discouraged. As long as you live within this world, you will face many hardships and difficulties. This is the kingdom of *maya*, My illusory energy, and her duty is to test the conditioned soul to see if he is cured from his madness of thinking himself to be the Supreme Enjoyer, God Himself. These tribulations are actually for your benefit and will ultimately help you to reach Me. Therefore, do not be discouraged or weakened in your determination for devotional service. I am with you, dear one, and will surely fulfill My promises to you, for I desire to reward you above and beyond all measure.

Life in this world is very short. Death comes quickly, My child, and then your sorrow is over. Be patient and wait upon Me, and you will see an end to all misery. My devotees easily cross over the ocean of birth and death and attain unending bliss in My abode. Do not weep,

My son. Whatever time takes away is trivial and as worthless as dreams or wishful thinking. It does not merit the grief of an intelligent man.

Whatever you undertake, do wisely and superbly. When it is done for Me and not for self, it endures the ravages of time. Devotional service is My superior energy, identical with Me. Therefore it is eternal and full of knowledge and bliss. Whether you read or write, sing or dance, cook or clean, worship or sacrifice, do it as an offering to Me for My satisfaction. Then you will know peace and contentment. By My grace, you will be able to bear great affliction, temptation, or persecution. To live in My abode is worth this and more, rest assured. Moreover, the peace that transcends all human understanding will soon be yours, though it will come at a time and in a place now unknown to you. At that time, there will be no more need for sun or moon or artificial light, for I am the Light of lights, and I will supply your every need. Neither will death and disease disturb you anymore, for I am the Lord of death and the healing herb. Anxiety and fear cannot enter that place, but joy and sweet friendship will be yours forevermore.

If you could only know the happiness of the devotees in My abode and the transcendental pleasure they enjoy in their loving pastimes with Me! They were once thought to be no more than simple village folk, but their love for Me was unsurpassed, even by multitudes of so-called great saints and sages. Now all souls bow down to them. You can follow in their footsteps. It is open to all: just surrender to Me utterly, as I advise. I assure you that all who heed My voice will come to Me and live with Me in the beautiful land of Vrindaban, full of cows and peacocks and waterfalls.

Who would not be attracted to such a place? Who in his right mind would prefer a few pleasant days now, risking unbearable agony in hell, to an eternity of bliss in My spiritual abode? Eternal bliss is My gift to the soul who perseveres in eternal love. In that spiritual abode I become the perfect Master, the faithful Friend, the most lovable Son, and the irresistible Lover. Whatever relationship of love you want, I will offer to you, My dear one.

Do you not long earnestly for this love? Does not this hankering penetrate to the core of your heart? Such is the nature of eternal love. In that love there is no complaint. Why care about trials and tribulations, harassments and slanders, loss of wealth, rejection by family and friends, sickness, even death itself, when eternal love awaits? In truth, the loss or gain of the whole world, even the heavenly kingdom, is a small matter in comparison to that.

Lift up your eyes, My child, and behold My smiling face. See the assembled devotees madly chanting and dancing in transcendental ecstasy, free from all anxiety, replete with devotion. It was not always so for all of them. In past lives many of them suffered many things for My sake and performed many great austerities and penances for the purification of their souls. Now they enjoy the fruits of that toil in pure love for Me. Now they eternally reside with Me, and I with them, never to part again.

☆☆☆☆☆☆☆☆☆☆☆☆☆☆☆

Meditation 84

Feeling Your Separation, O Lord

THE SOUL: O blessed home in the Spiritual Sky, illumined by the effulgence of Your transcendental body! Abode of bliss and Truth, impenetrable by the darkness of ignorance! O day of my Lord, bright and clear, changeless and eternal, let this brief span of time I now occupy come to an end, "for now we see as through a glass, darkly; but then face to face."

How short and vile this mortal life, full of sorrow and bitterness! Ensnared by passion and maddened by ignorance, we are defiled by innumerable sins. Sinning, we are subjected to the whips of fear, anger, hankering, and lamentation, and weighted down with the burden of manifold cares. We are allured by curiosity and entangled by lust, circumscribed by many mistakes and taunted by temptation, made impotent by pleasure and oppressed by desire.

Pray, my Lord, when will this nightmarish existence without You end? Who will loose the bonds of these senses and deliver me from the slavery of this flesh? Do You not hear me when I cry out to You in complete helplessness? Will You not fix my restless mind on You alone? O dear Krishna, killer of the Madhu demon, when will I move in true liberty, free from disturbances of body and mind, to perform uninterrupted, pure devotional service at Your Lotus Feet? When will real peace, undisturbed and secure, descend upon me? When will I hear ringing throughout my soul and throughout the universe, "Shanti...shanti...shanti?" O beautiful Cowherd Boy of blue, when will I be able to see You again, running and jumping in the forests of Vrindaban with Your friends and cows? When will I be able to enter into those pastimes of love, innocent of Your infinite opulence and power, completely captivated by Your beauty alone? Possess me, Lord. Ravish my mind and heart that I may be only Yours, and You only mine.

Alas, I am now deserted in a barren, hostile land, where daily we see war, pestilence, famine, murder, suicide, rape, and every other form of suffering and depravity. My banishment and separation from You are more than I can bear. O merciful Lord, help me in this hour of need. The solace of this world is useless. Apart from You I have no comfort. I want You, I need You, I desire to serve You eternally, but I have no qualification. Just when I begin to approach Your grace and absorb myself in the thought of You, another wave of worldly concerns and uncontrolled passion pulls me down. Although I desire to be pure and above all material things, this vile flesh forces me to commit sinful activities even against my will. Thus there is always a fight within, the soul wanting to rise up to unalloyed Krishna consciousness, and the flesh wanting to wallow in sense gratification. How unhappy I am, knowing what is right but powerless to achieve it. Even when I pray to You for help, a host of wordly desires rush in to devour me.

O Krishna, do not hide from me, and do not be angry with this lowly servant. Without Your mercy I shall perish. Disperse the enemy with Your glance, and with Your word, put to flight the phantoms of my mind. Only when You calm my disturbed senses with Your loving glance will I be free of all worldly desires. Fill me with Your grace, so that I may be full of love, joy, peace, compassion, and forgiveness and free from all vicious notions. Let no vanity move me, but make me pure, even as You are pure.

Pardon me, O merciful Lord, for innumerable offenses committed toward You and Your holy ones, for my nature is still very much conditioned by envy. I confess this weakness, which is the greatest of all faults, and pray that Your chastisement fall mightily upon me, lest this sin drag me to the most abominable hell. Wash my restless mind with the healing waters of Your Lotus Feet so that it may be cured of its filthy diseases. Very often my body is rightly situated, but my thoughts carry me far away. Truly, I am where my thoughts are, and my love is soon there too. I want to think of You always, dear Shyamasundara, Lord of my heart, and forget worldly pleasure and temporal love. Let my heart and mind be captured by You as easily and naturally as the affections of a young boy are captured by a young girl. Just as lovers never think or speak of anything but their love, let me think and speak only of Your wonderful pastimes and activities. Only then will I not be diverted to any other thing. Only then will my soul rest in You alone. This is my only prayer, my Lord. Please hear me.

☆☆☆☆☆☆☆☆☆☆☆☆☆☆☆

Meditation 85

Work Now, Samadhi Later

THE LORD IN THE HEART: When you long for Me and feel great separation from Me, desiring to be freed from the limitations and disturbances of the present body, know this to be My special mercy. Such anguish of soul is the surest way to experience My presence. Give thanks to Me for My unique understanding and compassion upon you, whereby I stir up your fervor and elevate you to higher and higher levels of love for Me. Left to yourself, you would gradually sink more and more into the mad pursuit of earthly pleasure. It is only My divine grace—manifest within your heart and in the person of the pure devotee and spiritual master—that awards this greatest boon of life. This is all to help you advance in humility and virtue and thereby in Krishna consciousness. Thus prepared, you will be able to withstand all the temptations of *maya* and cling tight to Me in all situations, serving Me in unalloyed devotion.

My dear son, sometimes impure desires arise in the hearts of neophyte devotees, just as black smoke sometimes accompanies fire. Such desires denote the adulteration of carnal affections. Still, although it is not always for My pure devotion that you pray so imploringly, I overlook the bad and accept the good. To improve, you should try to understand that desires mixed with self-interest are not pure and cannot give the perfect result. Therefore, My child, do not ask for things pleasing and comforting to the limited and temporary material body. Rather, inquire about the soul, which is part and parcel of My very Self. Think of Me and My honor, and in so doing, you will judge all things rightly and follow My will perfectly.

Don't worry. I know what you need and what you most desire, even without your asking, and I will surely bestow My blessings according to My infinite wisdom. Although you desire liberation and the freedom and joy of living in that abode where My eternal associates sing and dance, the time for that has not yet come. Now is the time for warfare, struggle, and tribulation. It is the time to advance My mission to save all conditioned souls. Wisely, you long to live with Me in heavenly bliss, but this is not possible for those who have even the slightest tinge of material affection. Purify yourself of every vestige of worldliness by thinking constantly of Me and always chanting My Holy Name. Then very shortly you will come to Me.

Have faith, My child, and be courageous. Be strong in Krishna consciousness, and put on the appearance of the new man. When there is a change of heart, all things become new, and things that were formerly hated are then loved; and things previously loved, then despised. Still, there will be many duties that you will wish to avoid, but for My sake you must perform them. There will also be things you desire but which you must forego for My sake. What pleases Me is always good and true; what pleases you may be false and therefore dangerous to you and others. My words heal and are appreciated by all, but your speculations are useless. Nor should you be disturbed when you see others apparently receiving more mercy, gaining fame, and achieving great success in My service. It is I who give and I who take away. I know perfectly well how to test My devotees and make them complete and perfect in every way.

Become wholly dependent on Me. Learn to see whatever happens as My mercy, and tolerate all things for My sake. Even those things that are inconvenient or useless by your standards should be endured gladly, just because I desire them. Such surrender is the greatest indication of love for Me. It satisfies Me beyond measure. It may be as bitter as poison in the beginning for you, but it is as sweet as honey in the end.

Remember, My child, that this life will soon be over. Whatever is done for the pleasure of the body perishes with the body, but whatever is done for Me remains eternally. The fruits of your present labors will soon be manifest, and you will not be disappointed, for your patience and surrender will reap the greatest reward. Whatever little thing you have forgone here will be returned with interest a hundred and a thousand times. There, in My eternal abode, you will find all that your heart desires. There you can possess every gift with no fear of loss, because there, time is no more. There, My desire and yours will be one, for you will desire nothing apart from Me, and none will oppose or hinder you, complain or stand in your way. There, all your desires will be fulfilled.

Submit humbly, My child, and bow to My will and that of My servants. For My satisfaction you should surrender to every trial, not considering who asked for this or who commanded that, or whether others are superior, inferior, or equal. Let it be your transcendental beauty that you fulfill the expectations of all. Let others receive more recompense, and let others reap the glory. Let others be praised and adored of men. But you, My son, seek only self-contempt and self-abnegation. By so doing, you will find My pleasure and My satisfaction. Make this your only desire: that whatever you do, whatever you eat, whatever sacrifice or charity you perform, in life or in death—that it may permit Me to be manifested and glorified in you.

☆☆☆☆☆☆☆☆☆☆☆☆☆☆

Meditation 86

There Is No Shelter Other Than You, O Lord

THE SOUL: Blessed is Your Name, O Lord, and blessed are Your words. From everlasting to everlasting You are good and greatly to be praised. You are the original Father of all, the eternal Protector and Guardian. Who knows Your ways, inscrutable and mysterious? As You will, so it is done. What more can be said but that it is good? Let all men rejoice in You, not in themselves or any other. Transcendental to this material world, You are the Supreme Absolute Truth, my joy and hope, O Krishna, and I place myself in Your hands.

What else can I do, my Lord? What do I possess that has not come from You by Your causeless mercy and without merit on my part? All things are Yours, for You are the original Creator of everything and the Maintainer and Destroyer as well. Whatever I have been given by You still belongs to You and not to me.

I am poverty stricken in every way, and my soul cries out in great torment. I can no longer enjoy a life of ignorance in sense gratification like the dogs and hogs, nor am I able to enjoy the bliss of spiritual awareness with You. Of all men, I am the most miserable. I long for a life of peace but find only suffering. Earnestly I seek You and Your light of consolation, but I find only dark, thundering clouds, and the beating rain. O God, take pity upon me. Without Your peace, I can never rest, but if You infuse me with Your divine love, my soul will be filled with joy, and I will sing a holy song in praise of You. Without Your help, O Lord, I will never be able to follow Your ways or fulfill Your commands but will fall into the most abominable hell, where, in separation from You, I will beat my breast and crawl like a beast. In such a state, remembering the time I stood in the sunlight of Your presence, I will beg for that mercy again.

O Lord of my heart, dear Krishna, in this dark hour of my soul, when I am sorely afflicted, protect me from forgetfulness. It is right that I should be tried in the fire of tribulation and tested by every kind of adversity, but allow me to remember Your love and compassion, Your wisdom and grace, and Your perfect knowledge and goodness. Then, although outwardly oppressed, I may inwardly dwell in the realms of pure Krishna consciousness. Let me be slighted. Let me be humbled. Let me fail in the sight of men. Let me be stricken with disease and misery, if it will help me surrender fully to Your Lotus Feet. All things are bearable if I can be ever mindful that You have appointed them and wished them to be, that You are truly the only arbiter, always in control, dispensing mercy, wherever, whenever, and to whomever You please, and that disturbances in this world are a boon given especially to Your friends and devotees, just to make them love You and depend on You more.

In this world, nothing happens but by Your sanction, according to Your inconceivable plan, and therefore with perfect cause. Thus it is good that I have been humbled and forced to give up my false pride and haughtiness. It is a benediction upon me to be shamed in the sight of men, for it makes me turn to You for consolation. Now I can understand that Your inscrutable love sometimes falls hard, like a thunderbolt, and sometimes it is soft and sweet, like a rose. In all circumstances, You are equal and just, awarding everyone his perfect due.

It is said that whom You love, You chastise. Therefore, I thank you, O most merciful Lord, that You have dealt powerfully with me, subjecting me to great turmoil, bruising me with bitter blows and manifold sorrows without and within. No one can heal me, save You, dear Krishna. I am bereft of every friend, resource, and defense.

Behold, O Krishna, my fate is in Your hands. I bow to Your discipline, and fall before Your correcting rod of affection. Strike me up and down. Straighten my crookedness to Your pleasure. Make me a useful servant according to Your desire—humble, tolerant, and virtuous in every way. Whatever I have, I surrender to Your chastisement and control, for it is better to surrender here and now than to be forced by the cruel hand of death. When forced, I receive no benefit. .

Nothing is hidden from You, O Lord. There is no need to inform You of current events. Give me the perfect medicine to counteract my waywardness and lead me on the upward path. Do not allow me to continue in ignorance, but teach me the ways of Truth and righteousness. Let me not judge a thing by my imperfect senses or by the opinions of foolish men who have no love for You, but let me decide with spiritual vision, distinguishing between matter and spirit, the temporary and the eternal. Let me heed the authority of Your word and the teachings of Your holy *acharyas*. What is the opinion of mortal man worth? Those who love this world cannot see beyond their five senses. How, then will they ever see You? Why should we care for them? Does a sinful man really become better by the votes of other sinful men? Can one drowning swimmer be rescued by another? This world is a society of cheaters and cheated, a place where the deceiver deceives the deceitful, the vain oppress the vain, and the blind lead other blind men into the pit. Here, men create their own hell out of disregard for You. Save me from this hell, O Krishna, and help me save others too.

☆☆☆☆☆☆☆☆☆☆☆☆☆☆☆

Meditation 87

Practice Humility

THE LORD IN THE HEART: My dear little soul, you will not be able to see Me always or feel My presence very keenly as long as the smallest sin binds you to material consciousness. The unbroken vision of My glory is reserved for those who have completely given up attachment to everything other than Me and My service. Even the great saint Narada saw Me only once in his previous life, and I granted him that vision just to encourage him in his spiritual quest. Even though he was only a lad of seven or eight, he gave up all worldly connections and searched for Me in the forest. When he finally found Me, he was awarded the benediction of being able to travel anywhere and everywhere, carrying his *vina* and chanting My Holy Names: Hare Krishna, Hare Krishna, Krishna Krishna, Hare Hare, Hare Rama, Hare Rama, Rama Rama, Hare Hare.

Follow in the footsteps of Narada, My child, and you too will become My pure devotee. But as long as you live within a material body, you will sometimes be subjected to the desires of the flesh and have to endure tribulation and heaviness of heart. How loathesome is this body of weakness, conceived in forgetfulness of Me, ever pulling you away from My eternal service and from divine contemplation of Me!

If you are anxious to escape from this bondage, you have to practice the regulative principles of freedom, praying for that day when nothing material remains, that time when there is only unceasing devotional service to Me. By performing humble acts of devotion and rendering menial service to My devotees, you will be nurtured in spirit and filled with unshakable confidence.

Now, if you patiently bear your exile and work for Me with great enthusiasm, I will surely come to you in due course and free you from all anxieties. I will wipe away all your tears of separation and relieve your fatigue of battle, and thus you will find rest in Me. Because of your implicit faith in Me and love for Me, I will reveal all the knowledge of the scriptures to you. Then, with an open heart and quickened mind, you will rapidly advance in Krishna consciousness.

Thus you will know that the sufferings of time are not to be compared to the glory that is yours in My eternal abode. Being freed from all material desires, you will know that you are eternally My part and parcel, that you are in Me and are Mine. In such transcendental consciousness, you will no longer experience hankering or lamentation—only pure love for Me. In ecstatic joy, you will sing and dance and chant My Holy Names. To such a pure soul, I am never lost, nor is he ever lost to Me. Together forever, we will exchange eternal love.

☆☆☆☆☆☆☆☆☆☆☆☆☆☆

Meditation 88

Causeless Mercy

THE SOUL: You are so gracious, my Lord, but I am not worthy of Your gifts. I am but a fallen sinner, ever forgetful of You. How can I obtain Your mercy? If You leave me impoverished and desolate in every way, I warrant it. Due to my many grievous offense to You and Your devotees, I deserve to suffer in hell for countless ages. Even then, I would be unworthy of Your grace.

Yet, it is the manifestation of Your infinite magnanimity that You extend Your help precisely when I am most fallen, unworthy, and undeserving. Although I was born in sin and have committed every kind of abominable act, You sent Your pure devotee to reveal Your transcendent reality in the miraculous form of the Holy Name. Thus You have consoled me beyond all merit and above material measure. In so doing, You have demonstrated the infinity of Your grace.

Men show mercy when there is cause, and they dispense punishment when there is reason. But Your transcendental activities are very different. You have shown me the greatest mercy and given me the rarest gift, but what service have I rendered, my Lord, that You should show so much compassion? Is it not a fact that I have done nothing good? Rather, I am inclined to evil, envy, and illusion—great faults that seriously impede my rectification. You know it is true; I cannot hide it from You. To deny it is to deny You, for You are the Witness of my heart, and to be without You is unbearable. Who would help me? Truly, for all my sins and rebellion, I deserve unlimited retribution and eternal separation from You.

It is good for my soul that You allow me this confession. I am most contemptible, so vile that if one of Your devoted servants even thinks of me or utters my name, he immediately becomes contaminated and sinful. Therefore, let me remain anonymous in the society of devotees. Although this is not easy to confess, it is better for me to expose myself for my purification and the sake of Truth than to be accused by You. Now, at least, I can beg leniency. Guilty I am, and full of remorse and confusion. I have nothing more to say but this: O Krishna, Protector of surrendered souls, have mercy upon me. I have sinned and fallen into a most degraded life. Pardon me, O Lord, and turn me not away. Have mercy upon me. I am Your child, weak and helpless. Indulge me a little longer while I pour out my grief, lest I fall under the shadow of death and descend to the darkest regions of existence, reserved for those who forget You.

What more can a guilty, wretched sinner do than humble himself and forsake his sinful ways? If, in true contrition and absolute humility of heart, he remembers Your Lotus Feet and accepts his eternal servitude to Your Lordship, is not the hope of forgiveness and reconciliation then born? Indeed, at that moment, in a second, cannot the troubled conscience of a changed heart be soothed and divine grace be found? To You, dear Krishna, sorrow for disobedience, proved by obedience, is the most acceptable offering, far sweeter than incense or perfume. You have never turned away a meek and submissive spirit soul. True surrender is the place of refuge from all sinful reactions. Indeed, surrender counteracts all the sinful reactions of countless material lives. Let me therefore take shelter of You, O Lord. Be my refuge and my hope, I pray.

☆☆☆☆☆☆☆☆☆☆☆☆☆☆☆☆

Meditation 89

God's Grace Is Known By The Pure In Heart

THE LORD IN THE HEART: My grace is very discriminating, My child, and cannot tolerate adulteration with material or worldly affairs. It is for the pure in heart and for those who are fully surrendered unto Me. Put aside all obstacles to My love, My child, and I shall fill you with unspeakable joy.

Do not be fooled by the illusions of your senses, but know the eternal Self within. Why do you seek the conversation of worldly men? They cannot help you, but they can do you great harm. Keep My company and concentrate all your attention on Me. Open your heart and pour forth your prayers to Me in pure devotion. Thus your mind will remain calm and your heart content.

If you are serious to advance in eternal love, you should consider the whole material world worthless. Service to Me must be your first concern, coming before any material occupation. You cannot please two masters simultaneously: either you will satisfy the one and displease the other, or you will please the other and disappoint the first. I demand total, exclusive love. You must be willing to renounce even your nearest and dearest friends and concentrate all your energies on Me. Then will your mind free itself of all earthly attachments and soar with Me in the absolute freedom of pure spiritual love.

If you live as a pilgrim and a stranger, unattached to this mortal world, you will be able to face the hour of death with peace and joy. You will know that death is nothing but My other face, welcoming you to My abode in the Spiritual Sky. However, the soul covered by illusion, suffering from the skin disease of bodily identification, never knows the bliss of a heart liberated from all other loves, nor the freedom of one who surrenders all to Me.

Liberation can come in the twinkling of an eye, and you can be completely spiritualized in a second, but you must see both strangers and friends not as objects of sense gratification but as objects of service to Me. Do not expect to help others until you have saved yourself. "Physician, heal thyself." When you have completely conquered your selfish will, you can properly assist others. Therefore, the real goal and ultimate victory is to subdue your own body and mind. A true *goswami* is qualified to be spiritual master of the whole world, because he keeps his senses under such tight control that sensuality obeys intelligence, and intelligence obeys Me.

My little child, if you aspire to this highest calling, you must begin now to cut down the tree of illusion, the tree of material desire. Manfully, with great determination, you must remove the very root, and tear out and destroy every trace of unruly love and earthly desire. Every vice and evil comes from mistaking lust for love—false love for real love. Love is meant for Me alone. Thus when your love reposes in Me alone, all evils vanish, and great peace and happiness ensue.

It is only because so many people refuse to die entirely to selfishness that the world remains imprisoned in dreams of birth and death and people are rarely lifted by spiritual awareness to the blissful life of eternity and knowledge. But whoever desires Me and clings only to Me, mortifying all low and inordinate desires, walks with Me in the beauty of holiness and the Truth of eternal love.

☆☆☆☆☆☆☆☆☆☆☆☆☆☆☆☆

Meditation 90

Opposite Poles

THE LORD IN THE HEART: Scrutinize carefully, My child, the workings of My different energies—superior, inferior, and marginal. Each originates in Me, but their movements differ. My superior energy, illuminating and liberating, exists eternally in the Spiritual Sky; My inferior material energy, subtle and illusory, deceives even men of knowledge, unless My grace intervenes. My marginal energy is composed of all living beings, My parts and parcels, who move under the control of one of the other two energies by their own free choice. All creatures indeed desire what is good and thus follow My path. Those under the superior energy know Me as I am and know the good to be in Me. However, those under the deluding inferior nature, thinking themselves to be this body of flesh and blood, find good only in themselves and in their own thoughts and deeds. Thus, there are ever two classes of men, the godly and the ungodly, each pursuing the good from opposite sides—one in Truth, and one in illusion.

The cunning and artful material nature tricks many into accepting this temporary creation as all in all and settling for self-gratification instead of self-realization. Thus it traps them in the vicious cycle of birth and death. The superior, spiritual nature, however, leads to the realms of Truth by way of simplicity and high thinking. Far from the paths of evil and deceit, it runs always to Me, where it ends in peace and rest.

Although materialists are not willing to die, they always die; although they are afraid to be kept down and overcome, they are always subdued. Learning neither self-control nor surrender to Me, they are baffled by a hard struggle for existence. Those under My superior, spiritual nature, on the other hand, submit to My will, strive for self-abnegation, and find self-fulfillment. Shunning pleasure for pleasure's sake, they work tirelessly for the pleasure of their Lord. Although they resist the influence of others, they remain always surrendered to Me, longing to be conquered by Me. Their love never misuses its liberty but accepts discipline readily. Not desiring to lord it over others, they aspire to be the servant of the servant of My servant and thereby become very, very dear to Me.

This world teaches one to follow his own interest and get as much as he can while he can. The spirit of superior love, however, never seeks selfish interest but what is useful in devotional service. This world longs for honor and adoration, but My devotees faithfully ascribe all honor and glory to Me. The conditioned soul fears contempt and shame, but those enlightened by My grace are happy to endure all things for My sake. In illusion, men love ease and relaxation, but a devotee hates idleness and relishes hard labor for My satisfaction. This world wants to possess things rare and beautiful, despising the common and coarse, but those whose minds are fixed on Me, seeing everything in relation to Me, take pleasure in even the most humble and simple things.

The flesh hankers for material wealth and earthly gain. It becomes embittered by even a small slight or a single insulting word. Singing of the eternal, the spirit is unaffected either by loss or gain, praise or blame. The mean man is covetous, taking more than he gives, and he is very fond of the conception of "me and mine." One liberated from the narrowness of bodily life, however, is kind to all and openhearted to friend and foe. He has no private interest and is satisfied with little. He is happier in giving than in receiving, for he thinks only of the supreme "Me and Mine."

Meditate well on these distinctions, My child, for you must choose whom to obey.

☆☆☆☆☆☆☆☆☆☆☆☆☆☆☆

Meditation 91

More On My Two Natures

THE LORD IN THE HEART: Hear again of My diverse natures, My child, for you are controlled by one of them.

Material nature thinks of creatures, its own pleasure, and vanity. Those who are bound by it run to and fro vainly searching for happiness, but those situated in My grace draw near to Me, to virtue and Truth. Renouncing all creatures and hating the flesh, they are content to remain in My house and serve Me constantly. Materialists are addicted to bodily comfort for sensual delight, but My devotees take shelter in Me alone and find peace and happiness in the highest Truth, not in things visible to material eyes.

The lower nature seeks its own gain and pursues its own interest. Nothing is done without pay or reward, praise or favor. The higher nature makes no such demands and loves not the things of this world. Content with whatever bodily necessities I supply, it asks no recompense but My service alone.

This world takes pleasure in friendship, society, and mundane love, praising men who never sing My glories. It is attached to family and takes pride in birth without considering death. It flatters the rich and powerful but neglects the weak and the poor.

Those who have taken shelter of Me love their enemies as well as their friends. They are not puffed up by birth or position, for they factually know that they are not the material body. Equally sympathetic to the rich and the poor, the wise and the foolish, the mighty and the downtrodden, they offer Krishna consciousness to one and all as the only remedy for the sufferings of this world. Thus they rejoice in reality rather than illusion, and love and serve My Person rather than My distorted reflection.

The inferior nature is easily disturbed, quick to complain, and always in trouble. It fights and argues its own case for its own interest. My superior energy tolerates suffering, returning all things to their source in Me. Being neither arrogant nor presumptuous, it ascribes no good to itself but acknowledges Me as the All Good. It is not contentious or attached to its own opinions but is guided in all things by the verdict of the holy scriptures and the holy teachers, who are My living Word.

The material nature is anxious to know many things and curious for news of various events, wishing to appear experienced and sophisticated for the praise of men. But My higher nature does not care for idle curiosity or news of this world, knowing that there is nothing new under the sun and that I alone am the beginning, the middle, and the end of all knowledge. One who knows Me therefore knows everything. For this reason, the superior nature seeks sense control, abstains from unnecessary material pleasures, and avoids praise and adoration, even for deeds worthy of honor. Knowledge, mysticism, devotion, service—all are tested by the utilitarian principle of usefulness to Me.

For My devotee, love of Me is a supernatural light, a special gift of mercy for drawing the soul back home, back to Godhead. It transforms matter into spirit, and mean men into saints. The more you hold your lusts in check, the more I give My love. Every day the reborn man is carried forward by newer and newer manifestations of mercy that bring him closer and closer to My eternal love.

☆☆☆☆☆☆☆☆☆☆☆☆☆

Meditation 92

I Am Unworthy Of Your Love, O Lord

THE SOUL: O Father, of whom I am part, make this divine love manifest in me for Your glory. Uncover the beauty of the spirit soul, now hidden in dark clouds of *maya*. Make me love You and desire Your service as easily and naturally as I now serve my unruly senses. Free me from this bondage to sin, O Lord, for only You can loose my chains and break the fetters of my heart.

Although I am a tiny sample of You, qualitatively one with You in eternity, knowledge, and bliss, I have fallen under the spell of illusion and become conditioned by corruptible flesh. Since the good in me has become a spark covered with ashes, I tend toward evil and base things. My ability to judge right from wrong, matter from spirit, is dimmed almost beyond recognition.

Thus, my Lord, I find myself in a most helpless condition. I see what is right and what is to be done, but I am powerless to do it. Instead of following Your instructions, I follow the path of rebellion and disobedience, serving sensuality more than reason. I want to do good and act in Your interest, but I lack the strength to accomplish it. At the slightest obstacle I balk and recoil due to fear or laziness. Thus, I am always miserable and despondent. The things that I know I should do, I do not, being weighted down by the desire for material pleasure and sense gratification.

O Krishna, Lord of my heart, I need Your love. I need that supernatural power that changes dead matter into spirit and allows me to begin some service to Your Lordship, render it in confidence, and finally see it to completion. It all depends on Your mercy, Lord, for without You I am nothing and can accomplish nothing.

Without Your love, O Govinda, what attraction can riches, power, beauty, knowledge, fame, and renunciation have? Anyone can see that Your gifts are bestowed equally on all, just as rain falls on both the dry land and the raging sea without considering where it is needed. Only when Your love is added do the opulences of this world become transcendental to material contamination. Indeed, without Your infusing love, good qualities fail to remain good, and even meditation and transcendental knowledge of the soul lack any usefulness.

O glorious eternal love, turning poorness of spirit into richness of virtue and offering the shield of humility even to him who is rich with many talents—be with me, I pray. Fill me with the energy of Your spirit, lest my soul dry up in desolation.

Grant me this love, O merciful Lord, for such love is all I need. Even if I am not blessed by the world but tried and afflicted with innumerable tribulations, I will feel no lack, nor will I fear anything in the presence of Your eternal love. This love is my hope, my strength, my counsel and help. It is stronger than all the forces of my enemies and more real than the power of illusion. It is more subtle than philosophy and wiser than wisdom. Eternal love is the handmaiden of Truth, the enforcer of discipline, the torchlight of knowledge, the comforter in times of torment, the dissolver of sorrow, the dispeller of fear, the source of devotion, the cause of enthusiasm, the sustainer of determination, and the object of tears. Without love I am a dead body, a severed hand, lifeless and useless, fit only for the fire.

Let Your eternal love, O Krishna, surround me and uplift me. Hold me tight in the hollow of Your hand. From that secure position, I will chant Your eternal glories without ceasing: Hare Krishna, Hare Krishna, Krishna Krishna, Hare Hare, Hare Rama, Hare Rama, Rama Rama, Hare Hare.

☆☆☆☆☆☆☆☆☆☆☆☆☆

Meditation 93

Deny Yourself To Find Me

THE LORD IN THE HEART: Listen to a paradox, My child: He who would find himself must lose himself, and he who would find Me must find himself in Me. By giving up the material or bodily conception of life, you will be established in peacefulness as My minute portion—in quality one with Me, but in quantity infinitesimal. Thus, you will learn perfect surrender to Me without hesitation or question.

Surrender is the hallmark of love. Whoever loves Me, knows Me as I am, the embodiment of eternity, knowledge, and bliss. Without eternity there is no existence, without knowledge there is no understanding, and without bliss there is no satisfaction. How foolish and unfortunate are the mental speculators and mundane philosophers who think that there is no absolute form and that everything is ultimately void! It is they who are void of true knowledge and insight due to their envy of Me and their causeless unwillingness to serve Me. Apart from Me, no one can exist, or know, or enjoy anything. How can something be present in the part if it is not in the whole? Just see how their intelligence is stolen by illusion. I am the beginning, the middle, and the end of everything; I am knowledge, the object of knowledge and the Knower too; I am unending satisfaction, complete and perfect in Myself.

If you sincerely wish to be My disciple and enter into My existence, follow the regulative principles of freedom. If you honestly desire to know Me, give up all mental speculation and fruitive activity aimed at enjoying this present life. If you want perfection and heavenly bliss, be humble on earth, abandon all varieties of mundane affection, and surrender to Me alone. If you abide in Me always, you are My disciple indeed. You will then know this Supreme Truth of Mine, and it will make you free from all material contamination.

THE SOUL: O Lord of my heart, dear Krishna, what You say is good and true but very difficult to perform. To give up all worldly affections and concentrate on You alone is not possible except by Your grace. Grant me that grace, O Lord, that I may follow in the footsteps of Your unalloyed devotees and achieve pure devotional service to Your Lotus Feet. This is my heart's desire. Nothing else will fully satisfy me.

THE LORD IN THE HEART: Yes, My child, happily do I grant you My grace, for I wish all men to return to Me in My eternal abode. My grace is manifest in the words of My pure devotees and in the example of their surrendered lives. Happiness, however, is more than knowing what is right: it is doing it. Like me, My child, you are independent. Therefore you can choose the good or the bad and whom you will serve—either Me in pure devotional service, or My illusory representation, *maya*, in sense gratification. There is no happiness in illusion, but in Me you will find perfect satisfaction. Only by pure devotional service can I be seen as I am, standing before you in this three-curved form.

THE SOUL: Yes, Krishna, I will strive for the good and try to serve You in every way. As best I can, I will meditate upon and follow what I have heard from You and the holy *acharyas*. Help me, O Lord, not to stumble and fall, not to look back or regret leaving all. Give me the courage to stand up and fight valiantly, depending on Your mercy, determined to bring everyone back to Your Lotus Feet.

☆☆☆☆☆☆☆☆☆☆☆☆☆☆☆

Meditation 94

Do Not Be Discouraged

THE LORD IN THE HEART: Have faith, My dear one. All the desires of your heart will be fulfilled. Do not be discouraged, even in times of failure, for what appears unsuccessful to you may be successful to Me, and what is meaningful to you may be vain to Me. Your judgements and Mine are still not the same. Patience and humility in all situations mean more to Me than loud chanting and feverish dancing without genuine submission.

To become saddened by some slight or by a little insult does not look very transcendental to Me. Those who are free from the modes of nature endure all hardships with equanimity. Why should you, knowing yourself to be part and parcel of Me, be so affected by worldly dishonor and abuse? This is a serious fault. Yet, let it now be forgotten. Such is the disease of the conditioned soul, for he is prone to mistakes and covered with illusion.

How long will you go on in this way, My child? When will you grow up and assume the life of a spirit soul? You act manly enough when there is no opposition, and you know how to give good advice and encourage others by fervent preaching, but when tribulations come to you unexpectedly, your good counsel has no potency. "Physician, heal thyself." Now is the time to consider your own weaknesses and conquer them once and for all by My power. Then it can be truly said that all things happen for your good.

Strong determination is required to cast every evil thing from your heart, to stop the desire for sense gratification—even the thought of it—for the mind becomes attached to and lusts after that which it meditates upon. But even when perverse desires are very violent, you should not be dejected or confused in your Krishna consciousness. Trials come, and in time they go. Wait patiently for My grace, and you will soon be delivered. Bear it willingly, even gladly, and do not become angry or speak rashly and offend others. Simply by tolerance, you can weather the storm that now rages. It will soon pass, and your soul's distress will be mitigated by My grace.

Be fixed and unshakable. Call to Me in desperation, "Hey Krishna! Hey Govinda!" Know that I am anxious to deliver you, My helpless child. Remain peaceful, but prepare well for tomorrow's test by girding yourself with transcendental armor—the constant thought of Me and the constant chanting of My Holy Name. There is no loss when you are severely tried; indeed, if you remember Me there is great gain. But if in that hour of tribulation you forget Me, all is lost. There is no hope if you neglect Me and the means of grace I have given you. In this world, there is no question of being free from all temptation, for you are a *jiva* soul—part of Me, but infinitesimal. Even great demigods like Lord Brahma and Lord Shiva are not free from temptation. But do not fear, My child, I protect all who take shelter of Me, and I bring to My abode all who sincerely call upon My Holy Name.

THE SOUL: You are so kind, My Lord, and Your words are like nectar to my ears. Your guidance gives light to my path, and Your chastisement lovingly urges me on. Anxieties and turmoil cannot deter me when I am encouraged by Your voice. With such a Friend as You, what need

have I for any other? I only pray, dear Krishna, that You protect me
from false pride and the consequent forgetfulness of You, and that You
let me remain always at Your Lotus Feet, chanting Hare Krishna, Hare
Krishna, Krishna Krishna, Hare Hare, Hare Rama, Hare Rama, Rama
Rama, Hare Hare.

☆☆☆☆☆☆☆☆☆☆☆☆☆

Meditation 95

Trust Me And Do Not Speculate

THE LORD IN THE HEART: Not all the mysteries of God are revealed to you, My child, and you should not waste your time trying to
figure them out: how or why you have fallen from the spiritual sky, what
is the special character of your eternal relationship with Me, why one
person suffers so much and another is greatly blessed, why one is so
forsaken and another so highly elevated. Such questions do not lead to
devotion but to speculation and disputation. They are beyond the range
of ordinary man's capacity to know.

When the mind is thus agitated or when curious persons ask, remind
them that the scriptures say, "According to their *karma*, or past activities, all living entities are wandering throughout the entire universe." What has gone before and what is yet to come are known to Me,
but not to you. Knowing past, present, and future, I deal with everyone

according to his need. I am equal to all and am fulfilling the desires of everyone. I am not friendly to one and inimical to another, although I appear to be, due to the imperfect vision of the conditioned soul contaminated with material desire. Furthermore, understanding the how and why of your position will not get you out, but surrendering to My Lotus Feet will. Therefore, it is said, "You fools and rascals, give up your mental speculation and dry argument. Just worship Govinda, worship Govinda, worship Govinda. Your grammatical knowledge and word jugglery will not save you at the moment of death."

Nor is there any use arguing about the individual merits of pure devotees—who is more perfect or who is more intimately related to Me. Such thinking breeds strife, not peace; pride and vainglory, not humility and cooperation. It betrays a lack of understanding of My ways and My saints' ways, which are rooted in eternal love and sacrifice, not competition for recognition.

Distinguishing between My devotees, or *acharyas*, on the basis of material characteristics—this one looks holy, that one speaks eloquently, this one is charismatic—is a matter of material affection, not transcendental. My devotees are pure and unadulterated because their interests are not separate from Mine. They never forget that I am the Original Spiritual Master and the Support for all pure devotees. They are pure because I am pure. They are glorious because they do not obstruct My glory but transparently reveal My greatness for all to see. Some are My eternal associates, sent on special missions on My behalf; others I have chosen and perfected by My grace, personally guiding them, sometimes through great temptations and afflictions, sometimes with great consolations. Now their patience and perseverance are crowned with perfection, and I embrace them all with eternal love. I have no other love than My pure devotees, and My pure devotees have no other love than Me.

It is far better that you humble yourself before these great souls and learn to serve them submissively. Through such sincere service, the Ultimate Truth will be revealed to you, and you will know all things good and necessary for Krishna consciousness. What more do you need,

My child? To hanker for more is to miss what you have. Chant Hare Krishna and be happy.

☆☆☆☆☆☆☆☆☆☆☆☆

Meditation 96

Who Will Be Great In The Kingdom Of God?

THE SOUL: I agree that my speculations are quite useless, but can't You tell us who will be great in the Kingdom of God?

THE LORD IN THE HEART: In My Kingdom all are great, for all are servants of the Supreme Great. I have made both the great and the small, and he who offends the least of these offends Me also. The devotee exists in the core of My heart, and I live forever in the heart of My pure devotee. We are all one, not without individuality—for individuality never dies—but united in eternal love. Having the same thought and the same will, we are one in desire. Love never stands still. It must ever expand. For eternal love, I have eternally expanded Myself into an infinity of souls, each equal in quality with Me but minute in quantity. You are one of these infinitesimal parts, My child, and are meant for My eternal love.

THE SOUL: O Krishna, Lover of my soul, be near, I pray. Teach me to love perfectly. Perfect love is possible only if You show the way, for You are the Origin, the Sustenance, and the Goal of eternal love. Others are loveable and things are lovely due only to Your presence. Apart from You there is no love, only lust and ugliness.

Therefore, sensuous and mundane men, who lust after their own selfish pleasure, cannot speak or know about that highest state of pure love. They delete and add what they like, not what pleases You. Without You as love's supreme object, the hub to which all subordinate parts are joined, how can there be oneness, or peace and harmony? Those who are strongly pulled by earthly affection and mundane friendship and act with vain imaginations can never understand spiritual love. There is a vast difference between the speculations of conditioned souls and the realizations granted to mature devotees by Your grace.

THE LORD IN THE HEART: You are quite right, My child. My words have entered your heart and found fertile ground. Hearing from bona fide authorities is the sure and safe way to advance in pure consciousness. Avoid idle curiosity and undertake to perfect yourself in the rudiments of spiritual life. What good will it do you to know who is greatest in My Kingdom if you are not there, or to know who is pure and holy if you do not become pure and humble and thus come to chant My Name without offense?

Meditate on the magnitude of your own sins and the smallness of your virtues, on the distance between where you are and where you want to go, and you will act more acceptably in My sight. Approach My saints with humility and beg their assistance in devotional service, and you will be more successful than those who uselessly try to understand everything by research and scholarship.

My devotees are satisfied in the Self alone. They do not take pride in the material body, or mind, or in their own goodness, for they ascribe every good and perfect thing to Me. In turn, I give all to them. Thus, they are so full of My love that they sing and dance in ecstasy and offer this love to others. No one is more dear to Me than one who distributes this precious knowledge, for I am very anxious to get all of My sons back home, back to Godhead. I request you too, My child, to become a preacher of Krishna consciousness and distribute My mercy to all. Do not consider who is fit and who is not. Give it freely, without price or qualification. Let My grace fall on all who chant My Holy Name: Hare Krishna, Hare Krishna, Krishna Krishna, Hare Hare, Hare Rama, Hare Rama, Rama Rama, Hare Hare.

☆☆☆☆☆☆☆☆☆☆☆☆☆

Meditation 97

Let Me Take Shelter Of You, Dear Krishna

THE SOUL: What is my hope, O Lord, and in whom can I trust without fail? When all attempts are unsuccessful, to whom can I turn? To You, dear Krishna, my Lord and Friend. Who else displays causeless mercy, unbounded grace, unparalleled compassion, and infinite, eternal love? There is no question of harm in Your presence, and fear personified runs far away from You. Poverty is riches when seen as Your desire, and this life is Vaikuntha when You take my hand. Your presence alone makes every place Vrindaban. You are my only hope, O Govinda; therefore, I cry for You and wander endlessly searching for You. Dear Shyamasundara, You are my life and soul, my hope and confidence. You are my faithful Friend, my Counselor in every decision, and the Lover of my soul.

You are different from all others, dear Krishna. Others seek personal gratification, but You have no need for selfish pleasure. Complete and full in Yourself, You seek only my eternal welfare and make all things work for my good. Even trials and temptations endured for Your sake are not onerous; they make Your devotee glorious in a thousand ways. Thus, You are not less in tribulation than in benediction, for You are all good, all true, and Absolute in eternity, knowledge, and bliss.

Who but a fool or an envious rascal would not place all his hopes in such a wonderful Friend as You? Who would not take shelter at Your Lotus Feet? Because of Your greatness, I surrender everything to You—my dreams, my ambitions, my love, and also my fears, my troubles, my grief, my sinful reactions. No one but You, my Lord, can bear this intolerable burden. Everyone in this world is weak and fickle in comparison to You. If You do not uplift me, shelter me, guide and instruct me, console and comfort me, who will? You are the original Source and Fountainhead of all things. Without You, even numberless friends and assistants are useless. In Your absence, the most learned books and professors can give no information, and no place, however pleasant and secluded, can give protection. Without You, the whole world is empty and vacant. You are, indeed, the Reservoir of all pleasure, the Possessor of all opulence, the Source of all life, the Ability of every creature. You are everything, O Krishna, and I bow down to You again and again. Surrendering to Your Lotus Feet is the greatest comfort and blessing for all spirit souls.

O original Vishnu, Lord of the universe and Lord of my life, I surrender whatever I have to You for Your service. I ask for no material benediction in return but for purity of heart and mind so that I may become a fit tabernacle for Your habitation and a foil to reflect and broadcast Your eternal glory. Grant that in this body may dwell only love for You and Your eternal consort, Srimati Radharani. Let nothing remain that might offend Your Lordships, but use whatever is of value for Your loving pleasure.

In Your infinite goodness and causeless mercy, look down upon and answer the fervent prayer of this poor servant now exiled to the regions of death. Protect me, I pray, from the dangers of this corruptible flesh, especially forgetfulness of You, and preserve me in devotional service to Your Lordship now and forevermore.

PART THREE

Chant And Be Happy

Meditation 98

Chant The Holy Name

THE LORD IN THE HEART: Draw near, My little one, and chant My Holy Name. I have made the way easy and the effect sublime. My Holy Name is transcendentally blissful. It bestows all benedictions. Chant My Holy Name, My child. It is not a material Name under any circumstance, and it is no less powerful than I. Just surrender to Me, dear soul, and chant My Holy Name. Do not be afraid: I will preserve what you have and provide what you lack. I will deliver you from all sinful reactions and grant you eternal joy in My transcendental abode. Do not fear, My child. Chant and be happy. I give you My promise. Just chant My Holy Name, chant My Holy Name, chant My Holy Name. There is no other way, no other way, no other way, because the only religion of this age is the glorification of My Holy Name.

THE SOUL: Your words are very sweet and wonderful, O Krishna, and I totally accept whatever You say. Since they are Your words, they are identical in all respects with You. They are also mine, for I desire to keep them always in the core of my heart. Your compassionate call enlivens my soul and makes me eager to approach You, but the remembrance of my sins and callous rebellion frightens and oppresses me and makes me hesitate to approach Your Holy Name.

You invite me to come confidently and chant Your Name feelingly. If I do so, the whole Spiritual Sky will open before me. "Do not fear," You say, "I will give you protection." O how mercifully such words fall on the ears of a sinner! Freedom, existence eternal, blissful life with You! But who am I, O Govinda, that I should dare approach Your Holy Name? Approaching Your Name is no different from approaching You. Even the controllers of time and space, the creators and destroyers of cosmic phenomena, are afraid to approach You. Yet You say, "Do not fear, My child, chant and be happy."

Who can understand this kindly invitation, this causeless mercy? But how can I be so presumptuous as to call upon Your Name when I have nothing to offer? How can I take You to my dwelling, where I have so frequently offended and blasphemed Your Name? Demigods and *rishis* revere You, even ordinary mortals fear You, but You say, "Do not fear, My child, chant and be happy." So simple, yet so sublime! Had You not spoken it, who would ever have dreamed it? Had You not come personally, who would have dared to believe and call upon Your Holy Name? Verily, You are identical with Your Name in every way.

Was not Narada, the sage amongst the demigods, required to spend a whole lifetime performing penances and austerities before being allowed to travel freely, chanting Your glories throughout all the universes? Did not Dhruva, that determined and devout child, stand on just one leg without eating or breathing for a long time before gaining Your audience? Is it not true that great saints and sages would meditate in the forests for thousands of years, controlling their senses and subduing the flesh, yet rarely contact You? Then how is it possible that I—a poor, lost sinner, a creature of corruption, hardly able to concentrate for half an hour—can rush bravely into Your presence simply by uttering Your Name?

O Krishna, O Keshava, O Narayana, O Madhava, O Govinda, O Vishnu, O Madhusudana, O Trivikrama, O Vamana, O Shridhara, O Hrishikesa, O Padmanabha, O Damodara, O Vasudeva—You have hundreds and thousands of Names, and each and every one is identical with You, fully potent, perfect in eternity, knowledge, and bliss. I accept them all, and chant them with faith and gratitude. They are Your

Names, and they are You.

Haridas Thakur, the *acharya* of the Holy Name, used to chant Your Name three hundred thousand times daily before taking even a morsel of food. Others have sacrificed everything, giving up their lives, to chant Your Name. O God, what a wretch I am! How little I do, either quantitatively or qualitatively! If I chant sixteen rounds, hardly twenty-eight thousand Names, I think it wonderful. Still, I spend very little time in purifying myself for Your Name. Rarely am I wholly recollected or entirely free from distraction. How ungrateful I am, how unappreciative of my great opportunity! Surely, in the presence of Your Name, there should be no other thought, no other desire, no other love.

Why, then, am I so cold and indifferent? Why do I not hanker and cry piteously for Your adorable presence? Why do I not concentrate my mind and purify my heart so that I can hear that sound of all sounds, that life-giving vibration that awakens the sleeping soul, quickens dull matter, and frees the spirit forever?

We travel far and undergo great difficulties to visit holy places, to bathe in the sacred waters of the Ganges, to honor the shrines of bygone saints and marvel at their deeds, but we neglect You here in the sanctuary of our mind and on the altar of our tongue. It is good to visit a place of pilgrimage, but we must hear submissively from the pure devotees there and learn to chant Your Name without offense so that we can come away with an amended life of renewed dedication and true contrition. Otherwise, what will it profit us? In Your Holy Name You are fully present everywhere, and You make every place a place of pilgrimage. Realization of this will come not by frivolity, curiosity, or sensuality, but by fervent hope, determined faith, and genuine love.

O Krishna, Maintainer of surrendered souls, how wonderful are Your dealings with Your devotees! How sweetly and graciously You manifest Your transcendental pastimes in their hearts! O Krishna—all-attractive one, attracting the hearts of the faithful and kindling their love—simply by uttering Your Name, Your devotees are filled with love and virtue.

Your devotees alone can understand this great mystery. Unbelievers and faithless persons, who are slaves to sin, can never approach You or comprehend Your glories. At the first sound of the first syllable of Your Name, great spiritual grace is obtained, all reactions to past sins are immediately forgiven, and the natural beauty of the soul shines forth. Indeed, the devotee may even feel his frail material body so enlivened by intense love that he sings and dances like a madman—simply from chanting Your Holy Name.

My Lord, You have made the approach to You so easy and so sublime; yet we show very little enthusiasm and attraction for Your Name. Our neglect and callousness are much to be regretted, for we have failed to take Your supreme mercy. Your Name is our only means of salvation. If we cannot chant Your Name, what is our hope? If we do not relish the consolation and eternal joy of Your Name, are we not dead stones? The whole universe is filled and maintained by the sound of Your Name.

Oh, the hardness of heart, the spiritual blindness of one who has no regard for Your Holy Name! It would be better had he never been born, than that he blaspheme or misuse or become inattentive to the sound of Your Holy Name.

Still, You patiently call, "Chant My Holy Name, chant My Holy Name, chant My Holy Name." Who but a fool or a rascal would not heed that call of love? Who is so blind to his self-interest that he neglects the greatest gift, the greatest mercy, the greatest benediction— Your Holy Name. Grant us, O Krishna, the intelligence to receive and understand this precious treasure of Your Name:

Hare Krishna, Hare Krishna, Krishna Krishna, Hare Hare,
Hare Rama, Hare Rama, Rama Rama, Hare Hare.

☆☆☆☆☆☆☆☆☆☆☆☆☆☆

Meditation 99

Munificence Fully Manifest In Your Name

THE SOUL: I fall at the feet of Your Name, O Lord, and beg for shelter. Do not turn me away, for I come as a sick man needing a physician or as a famished man craving food and drink. My soul is desolate and cries out in desperation: O Krishna, Savior of the most fallen, be my refuge and comfort. Your goodness and mercy are inexhaustible.

But who am I to hope for Your compassion or expect You to deign to come to me? How strange that a sinner should approach the Supreme Pure, or that You should condescend to live with an offender! You know me well, for You are the Lord of my heart, and You know that there is nothing good in me. It is therefore inconceivable that You should freely offer Yourself to me in the sound of Your Name.

It is only right that I confess my own weakness and unworthiness. The infinite kindness You display toward me is but another feature of Your immense love. I do not merit it, but You give it to further show Your causeless mercy and demonstrate more perfectly Your unbounded goodness so that greater love and perfect humility will be manifest in me. As You desire, so be it. Let not my unwillingness and sinfulness stand in the way.

O most sweet and merciful sound—KRISHNA! How much reverence

we ought to have, how we ought to give thanks constantly and never cease to glorify this Name above every other! Yet, how can a mere man adequately praise Your Name? Where do I begin? How do I start to serve You pleasingly, my Lord? How can I prepare myself, and what should I think when I chant Your Name?

To what can I compare that holy sound? It is sweeter than honey, more harmonious than music, more beautiful than the morning star, more illuminating than the noonday sun. It is the sound of the Name itself, however, that is its own best description and the best praise of all. Therefore, let me humble myself completely in its presence and remain silent before its sound.

Krish-na, Krish-na, Krish-na. Who can say how much nectar is contained in those two syllables—Krish-na? When the holy sound dances in the mouth of the chanter, he desires many, many mouths. When that transcendental sound enters the ears, he desires many millions of ears. And when the Holy Name dances in the courtyard of the heart, it conquers the mind, and the senses become inert.

Glory be to You and Your Name, O Krishna! I bow down and prostrate myself before You. Let me take the dust of Your Lotus Feet and the water from Your holy bath and thus feel transcendental happiness. Is it not a mystery that You, the unborn, unmanifest, unchanging Absolute, take birth on the tongue and in the heart of Your devotee, and grow and grow until You unite all in loving service to Your Lordship? You are the Most Holy, the Lord of the universe, the One without a second, the self-sufficient Philosopher, and the self-contained Master of mystics. Why do You come to me, the lowest of sinners, unworthy to look upon Your face? Why do you implore me, "Chant My Holy Name. Chant and be happy"?

Behold, perfect eternal love! Behold, perfect eternal compassion! Behold, the fullness of the Godhead in sound! How can I thank You and praise You adequately for such great gifts? Who can fully understand and appreciate Your mercy in blessing the most fallen with the greatest wisdom? How worshipable are Your pastimes, O Lord! How omnipotent Your power! How incomprehensible and infallible Your

Person, the Supreme Absolute Truth! By Your word alone, all things are created, maintained, and destroyed. How wonderful that You, the Cause of all causes, are contained whole and entire in the sound of Your Name!

O Krishna, Lord of all, possessing everything from eternity to eternity, be with me this day in this most sublime of all incarnations, Your Holy Name. Help me, O God, to remain clean and pure within and without, so that I may chant Your Name with a joyous and spotless conscience. Help me to surrender utterly to Your Holy Name, continually renewing my heart with devotion. Let me always maintain my sense of wonder in Your presence so that the sweetness of the Name may be ever new to me and that I may relish it more and more.

☆☆☆☆☆☆☆☆☆☆☆☆☆☆☆

Meditation 100

All Blessings Are Given To Those Who Chant Often And Offenselessly

THE SOUL: Blessed Krishna, blessed Name! I come to You asking for the life of the spirit soul, devotional service. You are everything to me—my hope, my strength, my happiness. My very being cries out for your ministration, for I am, by constitution, Your eternal slave. Without You, my life has no meaning. Without feeling Your presence, I do not care to live. Come to me, my Lord, in the form of Your Name and let me drink deeply and often this nectar divine. Without this life-giving refreshment, I grow weak and die. Your Holy Name is sweet music to the soul. By chanting without offense, I immediately become part of Your eternal glory.

Unfortunately, I often fall prey to temptation and become lax in devotion. I commit offenses against Your Name and suffer the pangs of separation. Cleanse my heart, dear Krishna, and renew my spirit. Kindle my soul with the spark of Your Holy Name. Let me chant loudly and with deep concentration so that I may not lose my determination and forget the purpose of life.

What is my position, O Lord? If I am beset with distractions and material desires when I chant Your Name, if I do not avail myself of this most marvelous grace, then what will become of me? From the tender days of my youth, my senses have leaned toward evil, not good; toward forgetfulness, not remembrance; toward personal selfishness, not divine service. Thus, I have no qualification for chanting Your Name, but even though I cannot chant Your Name perfectly, I have no recourse but to go on trying my best. Therefore I beg for Your mercy, O compassionate Lord.

If You want, O Krishna, You can make me pure, humble, and virtuous—worthy to chant Your Name. I cannot do it alone. Lift me up, my Lord, and take away this heavy burden of guilt. Shower me with divine grace that I may see Your transcendental form, taste the sweetness of Your Name, and know beyond all doubt that there is no difference between Your Name and You.

This knowledge is not born of reason. It comes from You. The Name is Yours, identical with You and Absolute in quality. No mortal can comprehend what You have done, but You reveal all these truths to those who surrender in love.

O Krishna, I come on the strength of Your order, with firm faith and without duplicity, with awe and wonder, believing in the potency of Your Holy Name. By Your causeless mercy and divine will, I sing Your glories and unite with You in eternal love—not to lose my identity but to find it in You. Give me Your special mercy, O Madhusudana, killer of the demon of doubt, and give me a special portion of Your favor. Dissolve my selfish desires and illusions. Fill me with pure, unadulterated love and allow me to render unmotivated service at Your Lotus Feet. Then I shall no longer hanker for a life of sense enjoyment but be content with You alone. Your devotional service is the greatest joy, the real life of the soul, and the cure for every deficiency. When I chant Your Name, my defects are corrected, my passions harnessed, and my doubts destroyed. By such service, I receive the grace to be steady in virtue and the strength to be undaunted in my determination to do everything for Your eternal pleasure.

O Lover of my soul, dispeller of my weakness and my desolation, lift me onto the wings of Your Name. Take me out of the depths of despair and let me rise to the heights of spiritual grace, cheered and enlightened from within and changed for the better without. I am cold, indifferent, and lacking in devotion, but when I chant Your Name, I become enthusiastic, blissful, and devout.

Who, indeed, is so stone-hearted that he can hear the sweetness of Your Name and not be affected? Can one stand near a blazing fire without feeling warmth or dive into the ocean without getting wet? Your Name is the very fountain of life and the fire that never fails. Let me drink deeply, my Lord. Let me taste the sweetness of that sound. Allay my thirst with at least one drop of nectar so that I may not wither and perish, and inflame my heart with divine fire, one spark of which can set the whole world ablaze.

Dear Lord Krishna, You have promised to preserve what I have and provide what I lack. What do I have to preserve? Whatever I have that is good has come from You and is therefore Yours, and whatever I lack comes from my own causeless refusal to surrender to You. Unfortunately, I have kept very little worth preserving, but I lack so much, O Lord. Due to forgetfulness of You, my heart is full of sorrow, and I am burdened by sin, afflicted with temptations, and oppressed by passion. Who will deliver me from this intolerable bondage? None can free me but You, O Lord. Only You are transcendental and uncontaminated eternal love. Therefore, I entrust myself to You, my God, with all that

I have and all that I lack. Whatever I have, whatever I am—it is Yours. Now You can do with me as You like. You can protect me, or You can destroy me; You can embrace me, or You can make me brokenhearted by not being present before me. You are completely free to do whatever You like. You are always my Lord unconditionally, but please, I beg You, do not withdraw the mercy of Your Holy Name.

☆☆☆☆☆☆☆☆☆☆☆☆☆

Meditation 101

On Receiving And Chanting The Holy Name

THE LORD IN THE HEART: My dear little child, happily do I come in the sound of My Name, offering Myself to one and all. I do not consider who is worthy and who is not. My Name is beneficial and relishable for all, perfect and imperfect. Indeed, it is purifying even to the creatures of the forest. Simply by hearing the transcendental sound vibration of My Name, everyone makes progress in Krishna consciousness. The Name should be heard from My pure devotee, however, for his loving recitation has the greatest effect on the hearer and will bear immediate fruit in the form of love of God. As far as possible, you should avoid hearing from non-devotees, for milk touched by the lips of a serpent is deadly poison.

Those who have been given the mercy of My Name have the greatest obligation to Me and to others. I have given you Myself, and I shall require the same of you, My child. Pay your debt to Me by distributing My Name to others, and thus show as much mercy to others as was shown to you. Become qualified to chant. By being exemplary and adorned with all good qualities and virtues, induce others to chant offenselessly. Woe to him who is a stumbling block to even the least of My devotees, for he shall suffer untold misery for many, many lifetimes. My representative is clad with devotion and decorated with My markings. His body is My temple, and he speaks only what I tell him. He sees Me everywhere and avoids the occasions of sin; he remembers My mercy and shows compassion for the offenses of others. He stands always ready to dispense My grace to all.

THE SOUL: I am bewildered, O Lord. On the one hand, if I do not chant Your Holy Name, I am lost; and on the other, if I chant offensively, I am condemned. What should I do, O Krishna? You are my Friend and Advisor. Please tell me clearly what to do. Teach me what is right. How should I approach Your Holy Name with true devotion for the welfare of my soul?

THE LORD IN THE HEART: My child, listen carefully to My supreme word: Above all other qualifications, I look for humility of heart and the sincere desire to surrender unto Me. Even the most abominable person becomes saintly by My grace if he is humble and surrendered. Therefore, with firm faith and pious intention, strive for the crown of pure devotion.

Examine your heart, My son, and purify your mind by the frequent and loud chanting of My Name. Be free from remorse and inordinate desires by taking shelter of My Name and be mindful of your every weakness and offense.

When approaching My Name, consider My extreme mercy in accepting you, even though you are still imperfect and prone to sin. I know your inclination for sense pleasure, your roving lust, your lack of sense control, and your predisposition for frivolity over seriousness, laughter over tears, a life of ease over a life of austerity and penance. I also know that you are slow to embrace renunciation but eager for opulence, stingy in giving but tenacious in acquiring, quick to speak nonsense but reluctant to remain silent, greedy for food but not for devotional service, prompt to retire but slow to rise, eager to hear gossip but unwilling to hear about my pastimes, quick to anger but slow to forgive, a good judge but a poor student, content in prosperity but agitated by adversity, good at making resolutions but not at carrying them out. Therefore, you are uncontrolled in character, sleepy and inattentive, without feeling and quickly distracted, unenthusiastic and unrecollected, and, most dangerous of all, neglectful of the proper chanting of My Holy Name.

But because you have a slight desire to surrender to Me, I overlook all these faults and fan that little spark of Krishna consciousness. You should be aware, however, that you cannot progress and become a pure devotee of the Holy Name if you continue to commit offenses. Feeling great sorrow and displeasure for these deficiencies, you should become staunchly determined to improve yourself day by day. Then, desiring to surrender to Me fully, you should offer yourself to My Holy Name each and every day, at every hour and every moment. Honor My Name, adore My Name, cherish it in your heart, bathe it with your tears. There is no better method for washing away the sinful reactions of countless lifetimes.

If you remain humble in My presence and do what you can, always chanting My Name, I promise to make you perfect and take you back home, back to Godhead. Do not fear, My child. Chant and be happy.

☆☆☆☆☆☆☆☆☆☆☆☆☆☆☆☆

Meditation 102

Sacrificing Whatever We Have

THE LORD IN THE HEART: My child, whatever you do, whatever
you eat, whatever you offer and give away, as well as whatever austerities you may perform—do it as an offering unto Me. Dead sacrifices
and useless offerings do not please Me, but the sacrifice of your body,
mind, and words is a pure and holy oblation and a living sacrifice of
love that satisfies Me very much.

I am not a poor man, nor am I in need of any material benefit. I have
created all things and am the Proprietor of both the material and
spiritual worlds. I am not attracted by the riches of men or the products
of mental speculation. I have no regard for the things of time, but I
desire that you surrender yourself to Me entirely. Nothing else can
please Me, for I seek not the gift, but the giver. Even if you offer Me
whatever you possess—yea, even the whole world—without giving
yourself, I will feel no pleasure.

Forsake all material considerations and give yourself to Me. Then,
whatever you bring, even the most humble offering—a leaf, a flower,
a little fruit, or water—I will accept eagerly. As I have given Myself to
you to be your constant Companion and Friend, so you should give yourself to Me without reservation. Giving is the expression of love, and My

eternal love resides in full surrender.

But if you maintain some separate interest and do not offer everything to Me, your love will remain incomplete and our union will be imperfect. Give up your rebellious will and know free will to be My will, for in self-will one finds only heartache and frustration. You are My eternal fragment, and when you place yourself in My hands without reservation or resistance, you become free indeed. Unfortunately, the conditioned soul does not know this. Under the illusion of *maya*, he thinks himself equal to Me in all respects. Thus he remains inwardly captive to My deluding energy, eternally bound and ignorant. Because he does not surrender to Me utterly and chant My Holy Name, he cannot know Me in truth.

Become My eternal lover by feelingly chanting My Holy Name. My Name is so munificent, that at the mere sound of it, by a single recitation, all sins are destroyed and pure, unalloyed devotion is awakened in the heart. My Name is all-powerful and not dependent on anything else for its efficacy. It does not even wait for initiation, or ritualistic observances. As soon as that transcendental sound vibration, "Krishna," appears on the tongue and enters the ear, the penitent sinner is freed, irrespective of his status or previous qualification. Like the dying Ajamil, anyone who calls helplessly on My Name—knowingly or unknowingly, directly or indirectly—is saved from the cruel hand of death. Thus, earthly bondage and cyclic rebirth are destroyed, and the seed of devotion sprouts in a new life for the soul, a life of eternal love with Me.

THE SOUL: Dear Krishna, I know that all things are Yours, for You are in every respect the Origin and Source of all that be. I long to be Yours, and to give myself to You entirely, a perpetual offering of love for Your eternal enjoyment. Let me chant Your Holy Name in a humble frame of mind, thinking myself no better than the garbage in the street and ready to give respect to every living entity without desiring any for myself. With a contrite heart, let me sing Your glories and magnify Your Name above all others as a sacrifice of everlasting exaltation. Accept this humble offering, my Lord, for it is all that I have.

Although I have nothing to give You but myself, I can at least refrain from falsely claiming what is Yours. In material consciousness we are always thinking in terms of "I and mine," but in Krishna consciousness we know that everything is Yours. Due to this false impression, I have commited many sinful activities and made many grievous offenses, which I beg You to please forgive and forget. Burn up my sinful reactions in the fire of Your love. Let my consciousness return to its pristine purity by the cleansing power of Your Name. Make it as it was before I ever left Your eternal abode.

What more can I do, my Lord, than chant Your precious Name, remembering Your great mercy and resolving never to commit offenses again. Whatever atonement You prescribe, I shall gladly perform. Treat me according to Your infinite mercy, not according to my rebellious and sinful ways. Grant me that new life of Krishna consciousness You have promised. Give me Your Holy Name.

☆☆☆☆☆☆☆☆☆☆☆☆☆

Meditation 103

Be Faithful In Chanting My Name

THE LORD IN THE HEART: Dear soul, if you wish to protect yourself from the attacks of *maya*, and remain free from the modes of passion and ignorance, always chant My Holy Name, returning constantly to the very Source of divine grace and mercy, the Fountainhead of perfect purity and goodness.

This life is a great battle for the destiny of the soul. It is your chance to be victorious and go back home, back to Godhead. But the enemy, the illusory energy, will try to defeat you in every way and keep you trapped in this material world. Well aware of the great efficacy of My Name, she tries with all her cunning powers and alluring tricks to prevent you from receiving the healing mercy of the Holy Name. Indeed, it may be that you suffer the greatest and most severe attacks while attempting to call to Me, for if *maya* can make you become fearful or perplexed or doubtful at that time and convince you to neglect My Name, you will gradually weaken and fall under her control.

Pay no heed, therefore, to her deceitful ploys, no matter how reasonable or important they appear. Know that every suggestion to neglect the chanting of My Name comes from *maya*, not from Me. Despise and scorn such wretched suggestions, and faithfully call upon Me and take shelter of My Holy Name.

Often the temptress tries to prevent you from approaching My fountain of grace by using the weapon of discouragement. Depression and lack of enthusiasm, perhaps arising from meager results or failure to realize advancement, are powerful enemies to be destroyed.

Again, *maya* may try to convince you that chanting My Name will cause you to advance too rapidly, to become too pure and holy, a state you are not prepared for and will not be able to maintain. "Go slowly," she says. "Don't be fanatical."

Do not listen to these lies, My child, but follow the example of the wise. Cast off every doubt and fear, every anxiety and reservation, and call upon Me with great determination and in complete submission. I cannot remain far away from one who feelingly chants My Name, nor can I be long absent from his company.

Do not neglect My mercy, but reject every evil thing that hinders your devotion. When vexed or troubled, root out the cause. If you have committed some offense, beg forgiveness; if others have offended you, excuse them gladly. If you have sinned, confess it to Me, and I will certainly pardon it. I do not delight in punishing sinners, and when an offender gives up offending and takes shelter of Me alone, I am fully satisfied. Show your sorrow for sin by forsaking it. Cleanse yourself of evil by spitting out the poison immediately. Quickly apply the remedy of the Holy Name, for it is always better now than later. If you neglect chanting My glories today for this reason or that, then tomorrow you will default for yet a greater concern. How sad that some avoid My Name, fearing they will be forced to give up sense gratification and control their unruly senses! Alas, what lack of true love and devotion is exhibited by those who are careless in approaching My Name! Such procrastination usually leads to prolonged spiritual sleep.

Shake off this lethargy and hardness of heart. I have made Myself easily available in the sound of My Name for Your benefit. Take My mercy, My child. Chant and be happy.

☆☆☆☆☆☆☆☆☆☆☆☆☆☆☆

Meditation 104

The Holy Name, My Only Solace

THE SOUL: O most sweet and wonderful Krishna, how fortunate is the devotee who feasts upon and relishes the sound of Your Holy Name! For the meager price of calling Your Name, You descend in sound and manifest the fullness of Your glory on the tongue of Your pure devotee.

O my Lord, when will my eyes be decorated with tears of love flowing incessantly when I chant Your Holy Name? When will my voice choke up, and the hairs of my body stand on end upon hearing the sound of Your Name? How do I obtain that devotion? I am like a dead man with a stone-cold heart. My whole being ought to be so ablaze with love that I sing and dance and leap for joy, unable to remain calm for a second. Though hidden from the world by clouds of *maya*, You have come to me, whole and entire, in the sound of Your Name.

How strange that at the same time, in the same place, at the same event, one soul sees You directly, face to face, and another sees nothing but dull matter! How inconceivable and worshipable is even Your perverted reflection, this world of illusion, which simultaneously covers the envious and enlightens the pious! Then what to speak of You, O Ruler of Vrindaban, manifesting Yourself personally, heart to heart, to those who have surrendered all to You and feelingly chant Your Holy Name?

O Govinda, primeval Lord, Shyamasundara Himself, I worship You, I adore You, I fall down at Your Lotus Feet, begging for shelter. Do not kick me away. Be my love, O Krishna, for nothing else will comfort me, and nobody can give me satisfaction or rest but You, my Lord. I desire to contemplate Your Lotus Feet forever, and unceasingly engage in service for Your personal pleasure.

Alas, such is not possible for me, a poor conditioned soul, full of defects and imperfections. But it is possible for You, O God. Although I am nothing and have no qualification, You, my Lord, can infuse me with Your divine grace and make me perfect and holy in Your sight. I believe in and wait patiently for this mercy, following in the footsteps of the previous *acharyas*, who attained perfection by Your grace. Besides this, You have given me Your holy books for guidance, and greatest of all, You have given me Your Holy Name as my special haven and refuge.

This world's miseries would be unbearable were it not for two things: nourishment and light. For the maintenance of my body and soul, You have given Yourself in the form of delicious Krishna *prasadam*—the remnants of Your food, prepared for You and offered to You with love by Your devotees. By Your accepting them, these foods are transformed into something transcendental and spiritual. Simply by eating the remnants of these foods tasted by You, my body, mind, and soul are at once refreshed.

Furthermore, You have illumined this dark dungeon of material life with the torchlight of Vedic knowledge, which reveals both of us simultaneously, eternally united in transcendental love. All these truths are clear to one who humbly chants Your Name with thanksgiving.

How fortunate is he who receives this gift, and how wonderful is he who gives it to others! No one is more dear to You than he, You declare, for he delivers You on the wings of sound to liberate all who pause to hear. How pure he must be whose lips utter Your Name, how hallowed his body, how clean his mind and sanctified his spirit! Indeed, his mission is to save all mankind.

Grant me, O Krishna, to be ever worthy of this high calling—to speak nothing but what is true and holy, good and profitable; to keep my eyes fixed on You; and to act only for Your pleasure, according to Your order. I am Your eternal servant. Now, I pray, make that service perfect.

☆☆☆☆☆☆☆☆☆☆☆☆☆☆☆

Meditation 105

Prepare To Chant With Great Care

THE LORD IN THE HEART: I am the Supreme Pure, and the Most Holy. In a heart made clean by the chanting of My Name, I take My rest.

The strength of your desire to have Me dwell with you will be shown by how quickly and thoroughly you purge out your old sinful ways and make spotless the habitation of your heart. Shut out all material considerations, and sitting like the lonely sparrow on the rooftop, meditate on Me.

To love means to give one's best. Thus, the lover makes every preparation possible for the comfort of the beloved. Love is recognized thereby. There is no preparation, however, by which you can truly merit My coming, though you labor for a long time and spend great sums. My mercy is causeless, a free and loving response to the love of My devotee. It is not what you have done that attracts Me, but the love with which you have done it. Therefore, approach My Name as a humble beggar who has nothing to offer in return, but surrenders whatever he has in humble affection, giving thanks to My Holy Name.

Make yourself ready, as best you can. Rise early. Bathe with cool water and dress with clean garments. Mark your body as My temple and prepare to receive My Name, the Name of Your beloved Master and Friend, not mechanically or ritualistically but in love mixed with awe and reverence. Do not fear Me, but fear offending Me, for it is I who have called you and come to you, and it is I who promise to preserve what you have and provide what you lack.

Remember, My child, I am the Supreme Personality of Godhead; I do not need you but you need Me. Out of causeless love I have appeared for your purification, your sanctification, and your reestablishment in devotional service. It is I who enlighten and awaken you to Krishna consciousness and show you how to live a life of holiness, united with Me in loving service. Use wisely My means of grace, O little one, and do not neglect My mercy. With great care, prepare your heart and offer it to Me with love.

THE SOUL: Grant me, O Krishna, the determination to find You and to open wide my heart exclusively for Your pleasure. Help me, O Lord, to be undisturbed by any creature or situation and to make You my only shelter, that You may freely speak to me, and I to You, without any hesitation, as a lover speaks to his beloved or a friend to his friend.

I beg for this, longing to be completely one with You in the ecstasy of love: to withdraw my senses from all other engagements than Your holy service, and to relish the celestial and eternal sound of Your most precious Name.

O dear Krishna, when will I be entirely submissive to You, absorbed in Your desire, my very self abandoned in service to You? O, heavenly dream, the lover and the beloved, the two made one, eternally separate, eternally united! Be my only love, my Lord, and let it remain so all the days of my life, for You are the greatest of all. You alone give peace and contentment to all who yield themselves utterly to You. Without You, there is only frustration, sorrow, and unspeakable agony.

How inscrutable are Your ways, O Lord! You are hidden from those who have no regard for You, but You reveal Yourself eagerly to the humble and the pure in heart. How kind You are to Your children, giving them the sweetness of Your very Self in the sound of Your Name. What can I give You in return for this boundless love and infinite mercy? I have nothing but myself, which I offer to You without reservation. Hear my prayer, dear God, and fulfill the yearning of my heart. Let me hear Your sweet voice reply, "As you surrender to me, I reward you accordingly. If you want Me as your Master, or Friend, or Son, or Beloved, I gladly comply. I am always in the core of My devotee's heart, and the devotee is always in the core of My heart." Yes, my Lord, yes, I want You to remain with me forever, and I want to continue this loving relationship in devotional service forever, for then I will never forget You or Your Holy Name—Krishna!

☆☆☆☆☆☆☆☆☆☆☆☆

Meditation 106

Realization Acquired Through Intense Desire

THE SOUL: Although You are so kind and give Yourself freely in the form of Your Name, I frequently miss the opportunity to chant and glorify Your Name, poor-hearted miser that I am. When I see others diving into this ocean of nectar and sacrificing all they have out of intense love, I feel ashamed of my coldness and lack of enthusiasm for this perfect gift. In the presence of such infinite grace, how is it possible that I remain so dried up and void of natural affection? Why am I not totally consumed with love in Your presence? O Krishna, my ever Well-wisher, why do I not shed tears of love and sing and dance uncontrollably at the sound of Your Name? Am I dead? Is my heart made of stone? I become confused when I see Your many devotees greatly eager to serve You, exhibiting ecstatic symptoms of love, and longing to embrace You, the Source of their life. They fulfill the burning desires of their hearts by the loud chanting of Your Holy Name. Their true and ardent faith, their great joy and devotional enthusiasm are convincing testimony to Your divine presence in their lives.

I long to have such pure devotional zeal, but it remains far away and eludes me. Give me Your causeless mercy, dear Krishna, and grant me just one drop of transcendental nectar to prolong my life and keep me from drying up and withering away. Allow me to feel, at least occasionally, the tenderness and love that You invest in Your Name. Let Your Name strengthen my faith and my determination to serve Your Lotus Feet unconditionally.

You can grant me this grace and enliven my soul, or You can leave me brokenhearted in separation from You. You are free to do whatever You want. In all conditions, You are my Lord and Master. I surrender to You. Still, I am hoping against hope that You will grant me this boon. Visit me most graciously, my Lord, according to Your infinite goodness and at Your own sweet pleasure. Although at present I lack the perfect zeal of Your unalloyed lovers and eternal servitors, I desire and long for it. By Your causeless mercy and boundless grace, even the basest of men and the greatest offender can be purified and attain a place amongst Your ardent followers. Number me also in their company, O Krishna, and do not send me away.

THE LORD IN THE HEART: My child, happily do I grant your request, but you must diligently prepare yourself to receive My grace. Seek it with enthusiasm, endeavor for it with confidence, await it patiently, nurture it by following the regulative principles of devotional service such as hearing and chanting, protect it by avoiding the company of ungodly persons, and know it fully by following in the footsteps of pure devotees. Above all, abandon yourself to Me, and leave it to My discretion to decide when and how Transcendence will appear.

When you feel your love for Me diminish or cool to lukewarm, become determined to regain My favor by sacrificing something for My pleasure. Eating only what is required to keep body and soul together, sleeping sufficiently but not more than necessary, speaking only what is truthful and beneficial, and working for the welfare of all living beings by advancement in Krishna consciousness are proper austerities for the body and mind.

Furthermore, you should practice great humility, thinking yourself the most fallen and the least worthy of My mercy, but do not become morose or overwhelmed with lamentation. Rather, fight for Me with full confidence, knowing that I will empower you to accomplish all that I have called on you to do. Always be mindful that in one short moment I can bring to pass what has long been denied. By surrendering to Me, Maharaj Khatvanga perfected his life only a few seconds before his death. Have faith, My child: he who perseveres to the end shall be saved. If My causeless mercy were always given at once or at your mere demand, it would not be causeless mercy, nor would it be esteemed by common men. Therefore, with humility, patience, and firm faith, await My supreme benediction—fervent devotion.

When this intense love for Me fails to appear, or somehow disappears, examine yourself carefully to determine the offense that has separated you from Me. It may be a small matter or something seemingly insignificant—if indeed something so offensive as to hide Me and My grace can be called small—but you must root it out and give it up entirely. When the hindrance is removed, be it little or big, you will attain your goal. From the moment you surrender to Me with all your heart, giving up your own pleasure and desire and placing yourself entirely at My disposal, you shall attain Me. This is the perfect peace and unity sought by My pure devotees: not the oneness of merging into My being, but the oneness of lovers, who know nothing as sweet and satisfying as the pleasure of the Beloved.

☆☆☆☆☆☆☆☆☆☆☆☆☆☆☆

Meditation 107

Follow In The Footsteps

THE LORD IN THE HEART: For your own welfare and that of all others, I advise you to follow in the footsteps of the great authorities of Krishna consciousness and chant My Holy Name without offense. Avoid arguing uselessly, interpreting My instructions according to your mundane way of thinking, and analyzing the glories of My Name with your tiny brain power. Such offensive mental speculation will plunge you into the ocean of doubt.

You should know that I can do more than you can dream of. I appreciate submissive and humble inquiry, and I reward the pious, humble search for Truth. To those who approach Me in a challenging mood, however, I give no help, but let them remain in the darkness of ignorance.

Blessed is the unsophisticated soul who presses forward on the safe, sure path marked out by My pure devotees, and leaving the dangerous way of speculative thought to the condemned.

Firm faith is the mother of devotion, and such faith is required of you, My child. A sincere and holy life is what I desire of you, not mere intellectualism or a delving spirit of curiosity. If you cannot even understand the mysteries of the material nature, that surrounds you, how can you fathom the Spiritual Sky that lies beyond the range of material senses and empiric research? I advise you to surrender to Me, dear one, and to dovetail your reason with faith in My words, that the light of real knowledge can be given to you. Then you will be able to understand all things, as far as such understanding is good and profitable for you.

Do not be vexed in mind, but present your doubts openly to Me. I have already slain the demons of douƀt, and if you bring Me their descendants, I will slay them also. Trust in Me and My pure devotees: We can put the evil enemy to flight. It is Divine Providence that allows My servants to suffer trials and tribulations. Indeed, *maya* has no need to tempt sense gratifiers and unbelievers; they are already in her control. But in many ways she tries the faithful to test their devotion.

Progress, My child, progress. Move on to new heights of Krishna consciousness with sincere and unflinching faith. With loving feelings, extreme humility, and great reverence, call upon My Name and shout My glories from the housetops. What is not immediately clear to you, commit to Me. I will not deceive you. But if you put faith in yourself, you will surely be deceived. I walk with the sincere soul, reveal Myself to the humble in spirit, and enlighten the pure in mind, but I cover Myself and hide from the haughty, the proud, and the envious.

The conditioned soul is weak, and his reason is easily beguiled. The transcendental Soul, however, is never deluded. Let reason and science, therefore, be subordinate to Me, and let them not try to supersede or oppose Me. All things are meant for My enjoyment, and he who would enjoy My company must learn to chant My Name in a humble frame of mind, thinking himself lower than garbage in the street, devoid of all sense of false prestige, and ready to offer all respect to others without desiring any for himself. When chanting is thus pure, faith and love emerge supreme and produce the most sublime devotion to Me.

If anyone, freed from other attachments, directs his whole attention to Me, taking shelter in Me alone by calling desperately and chanting My Name loudly, I will grant him My gift of devotion. When I find the vessel empty, I pour in My mercy unlimitedly. Thus, the more you renounce the things of this world and the more you die to the bodily concept of self, the more quickly I will enter in, abide with you, and ultimately, take you back to My eternal abode.

As soon as you perceive My presence in the repetition of My Name, you will know unspeakable joy and unending satisfaction. Your heart will marvel, and it will swell with eternal love. Because My hand is upon you, you will know peace and security unimaginable to mortal man. Therefore, My son, call upon Me and chant My Name faithfully, and I will bestow all My blessings upon you. Simply by repeating My Holy Name, you will be freed from all sinful reactions and return to Me, never to leave again. Come home, My child, come home.

☆☆☆☆☆☆☆☆☆☆☆☆☆☆

Meditation 108

Grant Us Eternal Love, O Krishna

THE SOUL: O Govinda, most magnanimous and beautiful Lord, whom I now approach through the sound of Your Name, grant me Your eternal love, now and forevermore. You know I am unworthy, involved in great vices, and often tempted, depressed, frustrated, and defiled.

In this whole world, I find no cure for my disease and no remedy for my suffering. Therefore, I am coming to You, the Great Physician, begging for treatment and mitigation of my pain. You know all things within and without, and You can help me if You so desire. You know what is good for me and what will make me whole.

Behold, I fall poor and naked at Your Lotus Feet and beseech Your mercy. Feed this hungry beggar. Revive my dead soul with spiritual understanding. Melt my stone-cold heart with the warmth of Your eternal love. Brighten my eyes with the radiance of Your face. Make all material things bitter to me and make tribulation and adversity attractive. Render all my lowly desires contemptible. Lift up my heart to You, dear Krishna, and let me not be diverted to anything else. In both time and eternity, let devotional service grow sweeter and sweeter to me. May You alone be my sustenance, my happiness, my hope, and my love.

Bless me with Your Holy Name, Your merciful presence in the form of sound. Wholly consume and transform me that I may engage in Your loving service eternally. Let me be united with You in eternal love, without any separation, O God. Do not send me away hungry and thirsty, but show compassion to me, as You did to the great saints of yore. Let me follow in their footsteps, always chanting Your glories with great faith and strong determination, with fervent devotion and ardent love, that You may manifest in my heart and in a life of pure devotion to Your Lotus Feet.

O my Lord, compassionate Krishna, my eternal Love, my ever Well-wisher, my Source of bliss and unending joy, I long to glorify Your Name, Your form, Your paraphernalia, Your pastimes—everything about You—as worthily as my predecessors in the discipular succession. Although I do not have their purity and unadulterated devotion, I offer You my heart completely, as if I indeed possessed those most wonderful and pleasing sentiments of love.

Furthermore, what little intelligence I have, I want to use for Your service. Whatever is beautiful, opulent, or pleasurable, I want to offer with great reverence and affection for Your enjoyment. Let me keep nothing for my selfish desires, but let me willingly, most freely, and eagerly surrender myself and all that I have for Your satisfaction alone.

O Krishna, my Lord and Master, I long to chant Your Holy Name with the utmost affection, with awe and veneration, with the deepest gratitude, with sincerity and love, with purity and worthiness. Let me follow in the footsteps of Your eternal associates, who chant Your glories continuously. Let me always remember Ananta Sesa, who sings Your praises and exaltations eternally with His thousands of heads, never reaching the end of Your glories. I long to be enthused with pure and holy aspirations and to surrender myself to You with all my heart.

Accept this desire, O Krishna, for it is all I have. Accept my promise to chant the infinite greatness and boundless compassion of Your Holy Name, as is Your rightful due. Let me chant every hour of every day, wherever I may be, that Your mercy may be ever with me. Let me not hoard Your loving kindness for myself, but let me invite all living beings to accept the perfection of Your matchless gift, which You offer freely to all.

ABOUT THE AUTHOR

Kirtanananda Swami Bhaktipada was born September 6, 1937, in Peekskill, New York. The son of a Baptist minister, he was imbued with the missionary spirit from earliest childhood: he would gather his playmates around him and preach to them. His parents took great care to teach him the values of Christianity, and he was a willing student.

In college, he joined the debating team, and showed great skill as a propounder of logical argument. Debate showed him that there are always two sides to any argument, and he began to wonder if spirituality could be limited to any one doctrine.

In 1958, he graduated from Maryville College, valedictorian and magna cum lauda. As a Woodrow Wilson Fellow, he worked toward his doctorate in American history at Columbia University. His thesis was entitled "Religious Revivalism in the Old South."

Setting aside his studies, he went to India in 1965 in search of a genuine spiritual master. His search was not fulfilled until his return to New York in 1966, when he met His Divine Grace, A.C. Bhaktivedanta Swami Prabhupada, the founder-acharya of the Hare Krishna movement. Here was the answer to his quest: spiritual life that transcended doctrinal concepts and led to pure love of God. He became Prabhupada's first American disciple, and, in 1968, founded the New Vrindaban community in West Virginia.

In 1977, Bhaktipada returned to India to see Prabhupada, who was about to leave this mortal world. Prabhupada requested him to carry on the discipular succession and become a spiritual master himself. Bhaktipada then returned to New Vrindaban, where he supervised the construction of Prabhupada's Palace of Gold.

Completed in 1979, the Palace—a memorial to Srila Prabhupada—has become a popular tourist attraction.

In 1985, Srila Bhaktipada inaugurated construction of the great Radha Krishna Temple of Understanding, destined to be the world's largest Krishna temple when completed in 1995. This ambitious architectural project has inspired both Indians and Americans and sparked international interest in the expanding New Vrindaban Community.

Srila Bhaktipada's special mission is to develop a "Land of Krishna" that will serve as a beacon of Krishna Consciousness for the world.